Bloom's BioCritiques

Bloom's BioCritiques

GWENDOLYN BROOKS

Edited and with an introduction by
Harold Bloom
Sterling Professor of the Humanities
Yale University

CHELSEA HOUSE
PUBLISHERS
A Haights Cross Communications Company
Philadelphia

Contributing editor: Amy Sickels and Aimee LaBrie
Cover design by Keith Trego
Cover: © Bettman/CORBIS
Layout by EJB Publishing Services

Printed and bound in the United States of America.
10 9 8 7 6 5 4 3 2 1

Library of Congress Cataloging-in-Publication Data
Gwendolyn Brooks / Harold Bloom, ed.
    p. cm. — (Bloom's biocritiques)
  Includes bibliographical references and index.
  ISBN 0-7910-8114-1 (alk. paper)
  1. Brooks, Gwendolyn, 1917- 2. Poets, American—20th century—Biography. 3.
African American poets—Biography. 4. African Americans in literature. I. Bloom,
Harold. II. Series.
  PS3503.R7244Z659 2004
  811'.54—dc22
                            2004012673

CONTENTS

USER'S GUIDE

These volumes are designed to introduce the reader to the life and work of the world's literary masters. Each volume begins with Harold Bloom's essay "The Work in the Writer" and a volume-specific introduction also written by Professor Bloom. Following these unique introductions is an engaging biography that discusses the major life events and important literary accomplishments of the author under consideration.

Furthermore, each volume includes an original critique that not only traces the themes, symbols, and ideas apparent in the author's works, but strives to put those works into a cultural and historical perspective. In addition to the original critique is a brief selection of significant critical essays previously published on the author and his or her works followed by a concise and informative chronology of the writer's life. Finally, each volume concludes with a bibliography of the writer's works, a list of additional readings, and an index of important themes and ideas.

HAROLD BLOOM

The Work in the Writer

Literary biography found its masterpiece in James Boswell's *Life of Samuel Johnson*. Boswell, when he treated Johnson's writings, implicitly commented upon Johnson as found in his work, even as in the great critic's life. Modern instances of literary biography, such as Richard Ellmann's lives of W.B. Yeats, James Joyce, and Oscar Wilde, essentially follow in Boswell's pattern.

That the writer somehow is in the work, we need not doubt, though with William Shakespeare, writer-of-writers, we almost always need to rely upon pure surmise. The exquisite rancidities of the Problem Plays or Dark Comedies seem to express an extraordinary estrangement of Shakespeare from himself. When we read or attend *Troilus and Cressida* and *Measure for Measure*, we may be startled by particular speeches of Ulysses in the first play, or of Vincentio in the second. These speeches, of Ulysses upon hierarchy or upon time, or of Duke Vincentio upon death, are too strong either for their contexts or for the characters of their speakers. The same phenomenon occurs with Parolles, the military impostor of *All's Well That Ends Well*. Utterly disgraced, he nevertheless affirms: "Simply the thing I am / Shall make me live."

In Shakespeare, more even than in his peers, Dante and Cervantes, meaning always starts itself again through excess or overflow. The strongest of Shakespeare's creatures—Falstaff, Hamlet, Iago, Lear, Cleopatra—have an exuberance that is fiercer than their plays can contain. If Ben Jonson was at all correct in his complaint that "Shakespeare wanted art," it could have been only in a sense that he may not have intended. Where do the personalities of Falstaff or Hamlet touch a limit? What was it in Shakespeare that made *Hamlet* and the two parts of *Henry IV* into "plays unlimited"? Neither Falstaff nor Hamlet will be stopped: their wit, their beautiful, laughing speech, their intensity of being—all these are virtually infinite.

In what ways do Falstaff and Hamlet manifest the writer in the work? Evidently, we can never know, or know enough to answer with any authority. But what would happen if we reversed the question, and asked: How did the work form the writer, Shakespeare?

Of Shakespeare's inwardness, his biography tells us nothing. And yet, to an astonishing extent, Shakespeare created our inwardness. At the least, we can speculate that Shakespeare so lived his life as to conceal the depths of his nature, particularly as he rather prematurely aged. We do not have Shakespeare on Shakespeare, as any good reader of the Sonnets comes to realize: they do not constitute a key that unlocks his heart. No sequence of sonnets could be less confessional or more powerfully detached from the poet's self.

The German poet and universal genius, Goethe, affords a superb contrast to Shakespeare. Of Goethe's life, we know more than everything; I wonder sometimes if we know as much about Napoleon or Freud or any other human being who ever has lived, as we know about Goethe. Everywhere, we can find Goethe in his work, so much so that Goethe seems to crowd the writing out, just as Byron and Oscar Wilde seem to usurp their own literary accomplishments. Goethe, cunning beyond measure, nevertheless invested a rival exuberance in his greatest works that could match his personal charisma. The sublime outrageousness of the Second Part of *Faust*, or of the greater lyric and meditative poems, forms a Counter-Sublime to Goethe's own daemonic intensity.

Goethe was fascinated by the daemonic in himself; we can doubt that Shakespeare had any such interests. Evidently, Shakespeare abandoned his acting career just before he composed *Measure for Measure* and *Othello*. I surmise that the egregious interventions by Vincentio and Iago displace the actor's energies into a new kind of mischief-making, a fresh opening to a subtler playwriting-within-the-play.

But what had opened Shakespeare to this new awareness? The answer is the work in the writer, *Hamlet* in Shakespeare. One can go further: it was not so much the play, *Hamlet*, as the character Hamlet, who changed Shakespeare's art forever.

Hamlet's personality is so large and varied that it rivals Goethe's own. Ironically Goethe's Faust, his Hamlet, has no personality at all, and is as colorless as Shakespeare himself seems to have chosen to be. Yet nothing could be more colorful than the Second Part of *Faust*, which is peopled by an astonishing array of monsters, grotesque devils and classical ghosts.

A contrast between Shakespeare and Goethe demonstrates that in each—but in very different ways—we can better find the work in the person, than we can discover that banal entity, the person in the work. Goethe to many of his contemporaries seemed to be a mortal god. Shakespeare, so far as we know, seemed an affable, rather ordinary fellow, who aged early and became somewhat withdrawn. Yet Faust, though Mephistopheles battles for his soul, is hardly worth the trouble unless you take him as an idea and not as a person. Hamlet is nearly every-idea-in-one, but he is precisely a personality and a person.

Would Hamlet be so astonishingly persuasive if his father's ghost did not haunt him? Falstaff is more alive than Prince Hal, who says that the devil haunts him in the shape of an old fat man. Three years before composing the final *Hamlet*, Shakespeare invented Falstaff, who then never ceased to haunt his creator. Falstaff and Hamlet may be said to best represent the work in the writer, because their influence upon Shakespeare was prodigious. W.H. Auden accurately observed that Falstaff possesses infinite energy: never tired, never bored, and absolutely both witty and happy until Hal's rejection destroys him. Hamlet too has infinite energy, but in him it is more curse than blessing.

Falstaff and Hamlet can be said to occupy the roles in Shakespeare's invented world that Sancho Panza and Don Quixote possess in Cervantes's. Shakespeare's plays from 1610 on (starting with *Twelfth Night*) are thus analogous to the Second Part of Cervantes's epic novel. Sancho and the Don overtly jostle Cervantes for authorship in the Second Part, even as Cervantes battles against the impostor who has pirated a continuation of his work. As a dramatist, Shakespeare manifests the work in the writer more indirectly. Falstaff's prose genius is revived in the scapegoating of Malvolio by Maria and Sir Toby Belch, while Falstaff's darker insights are developed by Feste's melancholic wit. Hamlet's intellectual resourcefulness, already deadly, becomes poisonous in Iago and in Edmund. Yet we have not crossed into the deeper abysses of the work in the writer in later Shakespeare.

No fictive character, before or since, is Falstaff's equal in self-trust. Sir John, whose delight in himself is contagious, has total confidence both in his self-awareness and in the resources of his language. Hamlet, whose self is as strong, and whose language is as copious, nevertheless distrusts both the self and language. Later Shakespeare is, as it were, much under the influence both of Falstaff and of Hamlet, but they tug him in opposite directions. Shakespeare's own copiousness of language is well-nigh incredible: a vocabulary in excess of twenty-one thousand words, almost eighteen hundred of which he coined himself. And of his word-hoard, nearly half are used only once each, as though the perfect setting for each had been found, and need not be repeated. Love for language and faith in language are Falstaffian attributes. Hamlet will darken both that love and that faith in Shakespeare, and perhaps the Sonnets can best be read as Falstaff and Hamlet counterpointing against one another.

Can we surmise how aware Shakespeare was of Falstaff and Hamlet, once they had played themselves into existence? *Henry IV, Part I* appeared in six quarto editions during Shakespeare's lifetime; *Hamlet* possibly had four. Falstaff and Hamlet were played again and again at the Globe, but Shakespeare knew also that they were being read, and he must have had contact with some of those readers. What would it have been like to discuss Falstaff or Hamlet with one of their early readers (presumably also part of their audience at the Globe), if you were the creator of such demiurges? The question would seem nonsensical to most Shakespeare scholars, but then these days they tend to be either ideologues or moldy figs. How can we recover the uncanniness of Falstaff and of Hamlet, when they now have become so familiar?

A writer's influence upon himself is an unexplored problem in criticism, but such an influence is never free from anxieties. The biocritical problem (which this series attempts to explore) can be divided into two areas, difficult to disengage fully. Accomplished works affect the author's life, and also affect her subsequent writings. It is simpler for me to surmise the effect of *Mrs. Dalloway* and *To the Lighthouse* upon Woolf's late *Between the Acts*, than it is to relate Clarissa Dalloway's suicide and Lily Briscoe's capable endurance in art to the tragic death and complex life of Virginia Woolf.

There are writers whose lives were so vivid that they seem sometimes to obscure the literary achievement: Byron, Wilde, Malraux, Hemingway. But most major Western writers do not live that exuberantly, and the greatest of all, Shakespeare, sometimes appears to have adopted the personal mask of colorlessness. And yet there are heroes of literature who struggled titanically with their own eras—Tolstoy, Milton, Victor Hugo—who nevertheless matter more for their works than their lives.

There are great figures—Emily Dickinson, Wallace Stevens, Willa Cather—who seem to have had so little of the full intensity of life when compared to the vitality of their work, that we might almost speak of the work in the work, rather than even of the work in a person. Emily Brontë might well be the extreme instance of such a visionary, surpassing William Blake in that one regard.

I conclude this general introduction to a series of literary bio-critiques by stating a tentative formula or principle for gauging the many ways in which the work influences the person and her subsequent, later work. Our influence upon ourselves is always related to the Shakespearean invention of self-overhearing, which I have written about in several other contexts. Life, as well as poetry and prose, is overheard rather than simply heard. The writer listens to herself as though she were somebody else, and the will to change begins to operate. The forces that live in us include the prior work we have done, and the dreams and waking visions that evade our dismissals.

HAROLD BLOOM

Introduction

Gwendolyn Brooks (1917–2000) lived a long and distinguished life, marked by her continuous devotion to writing the poetry of her people. With Brooks, locating the work in writer is difficult if only because her work after 1967 is very different from her poems composed before she turned fifty. Gwendolyn Brooks says of her pre-1967 poetry: "I wasn't writing consciously with the idea that blacks *must address* blacks, *must write* about blacks." I prefer the earlier achievement, a judgment (if it is one) that is harmless since much criticism already centers upon the later Brooks. Her early poem "The Mother" remains an impressive dramatic monologue, restrained alike in its pathos and its irony, and curiously wrought in emotional contraries:

> Abortions will not let you forget.
> You remember the children you got that you did not get,
> The damp small pulps with a little or with no hair,
> The singers and workers that never handled the air.
> You will never neglect or beat
> Them, or silence or buy with a sweet.
> You will never wind up the sucking-thumb
> Or scuttle off ghosts that come.
> You will never leave them, controlling your luscious sigh,
> Return for a snack of them, with gobbling mother-eye.

It is difficult to describe the effective balance of this chant. What precisely is the speaker's attitude towards her unborn children? Handling

1

the air is very different for "singers and workers," and the imagery of "luscious," "snack," and "gobbling" turns upon an implicit critique of the speaker's narcissism, while still expressing her implicit loss.

It is the second verse-paragraph that achieves a more disturbing level of intensity, in which something like a lament rises (though very obliquely) for those never allowed to be:

> You were born, you had body, you died.
> It is just that you never giggled or planned or cried.

A dispassionate lament is an irony, and so is the poem's conclusion:

> Believe me, I loved you all.
> Believe me, I knew you, though faintly, and I loved, I loved you all.

Another of her earlier poems, the famous lyric "The Bean Eaters," ironically and memorably celebrates

> Two who are Mostly Good,
> Two who have lived their day,
> But keep on putting on their clothes
> And putting things away.

This wry turn upon the universal still seems to me Brooks's strength, as does "The Crazy Woman," an eloquent extension of the Mad Song tradition:

> I'll wait until November.
> That is the time for me.
> I'll go out in the frosty dark
> And sing most terribly.

Brooks later became a poet of social protest, joining in the principal currents of African-American poetry in the last third of the twentieth century. She became more direct, and doubtless a liberating force. If I contrast her earlier poems with a poem of 1969, "The Riot," I come to see that I am not yet competent to judge the poet who was reborn in 1967. The satiric eye is still there, and the dominant stylistic influence remains T.S. Eliot. Yet the style and the stance seem not to cohere:

> Because the Poor were sweaty and unpretty
> (not like Two Dainty Negroes in Winnetka)
> and they were coming toward him in rough ranks.
> In seas. In windsweep. They were black and loud.
> And not detainable. And not discreet.

I like that "In seas. In windsweep," and I grant that the poem's sentiments are admirable, if you believe (as most of us really do) that only violence is the valid answer to violence. The difficulty here, as in the celebrated ballad the "Anniad," is that Brooks risks becoming a Period Piece, at some later time when American society has progressed beyond its long history of injustice. Ideological verse remains ideological; its paradoxes flatten out too easily. The enigmas of her earlier poems, like "The Mother" and "The Bean Eaters," to me seem imaginatively richer. Gwendolyn Brooks is acclaimed for her self-transformations, but whether she has sacrificed part of her gift to an exemplary cause seems to me a legitimate question.

AMY SICKELS

Biography of Gwendolyn Brooks

POLITICAL TRANSFORMATION

For the first twenty years of her career, the audience for Gwendolyn Brooks's poetry was made up of "chiefly whites" (Lewis 176). Then, when she was fifty years old, Brooks underwent a transformation that affected her political convictions and her poetry. Beginning in 1967, the author began actively directing her work toward the black community.[1] For the rest of her career, she followed the guiding principle that "Black poetry is poetry written by blacks, about blacks, to blacks" (interview 1988).

Considering herself an integrationist during the 1940s and 1950s, Brooks felt hopeful that soon African Americans would obtain full equality and freedom in America. As the Civil Rights Movement gained momentum, it also came under vicious attack, with church bombings and lynchings taking the lives of African Americans. The 1960s, despite significant gains made by the Civil Rights Movement, proved an extremely turbulent and volatile decade: President Kennedy was assassinated, as were activists Malcolm X and Martin Luther King; the Vietnam War had incited many protests and demonstrations; and African Americans were struggling for recognition and equality. It was a decade of activism, with people all across the country deeply committed to making changes in society.

Under these conditions, in the year 1967, Gwendolyn Brooks attended the second Black Writers Conference at Fisk University in

Nashville, Tennessee. The writer's conference, which concerned the theme "The Black Writer and Human Rights," included such writers as poet Amiri Baraka (formerly LeRoi Jones), historian Lerone Bennett, poet Larry Neal, playwright Ron Milner, editor Hoyt Fuller, and poet Haki R. Madhubuti (formerly Don L. Lee). Brooks went to the conference directly after giving a reading at South Dakota State College, where she was warmly received by an all-white audience. With the black audience at Fisk, she felt that she was "coldly Respected" (*Part One* 84).

As the speakers lectured and read their work, the energy level in the room increased, and Brooks felt as if she had entered "some inscrutable and uncomfortable wonderland" (*Part One* 85). As she explains in her autobiography, "Yet, although almost secretly, I had always felt that to be black was good," she realized she had never experienced this overt emphasis on black pride and solidarity (84). She felt immediately enveloped by the mood of the conference: "First, I was aware of a general energy, an electricity, in look, walk, speech, *gesture* of the young blackness I saw all around me" (84).

Like many of the audience members and conference presenters, Brooks felt astonishment at the conference's passionate emphasis on black autonomy instead of integration: "I didn't know what to make of what surrounded me, of what without sureness began almost immediately to invade me" (85). The calls of Martin Luther King, for blacks and whites to live in integrated harmony, were transforming into a social movement that advocated independent development of political and social institutions for African Americans, without support or interference from white society. The Black Arts Movement, while promoting artistic and literary development, also promoted the idea of black separatism. The movement, based on the cultural politics of black nationalism, helped to form black publishing houses, theatre troupes, and poetry readings. The majority of the literature of the Black Arts Movement, often composed in Black English Vernacular and sometimes confrontational in tone, addressed such issues as institutionalized racism, interracial tension, African heritage, and political awareness of African Americans in the United States.

The conference at Fisk introduced Gwendolyn to some of the most prominent activists of the Black Arts Movement. She recalled Baraka yelling, "Up against the wall, white man!" while Ron Milner accompanied him with "intoxicating drum-beats." As the energy level intensified and stirred the audience, a young white man jumped up, screaming, "Yeah! Yeah! Up against the wall, Brother! Kill 'em all! Kill 'em all!" (85)

Gwendolyn felt filled with a new passion, and believed her eyes had been opened. "You can't stop growing—I'm growing now. I have certainly changed from where I was back in only 1967," she explained. "I knew there were injustices, and I wrote about them, but I didn't know what was behind them" (Lewis 175). She felt the conference had presented her with a deeper understanding of racism and the opportunity to help advocate black unity.

When she returned to Chicago, Brooks became involved in running a poetry workshop for gang members. She also worked with and developed close ties to a group of young aspiring poets, most of whom were part of the black revolution. Once too shy to participate in interviews, Brooks now became adamantly outspoken about the changes in her politics. She no longer believed in integration, she explained, but instead was fully committed to black unity. Through her relentless advocacy for the African-American community, and for her dedication to her poetry and its audience, Brooks became one of the most visible participants in the Black Arts Movement.

Although many critics have focused on how Brooks's radical politics affected her poetry after 1967, with various critics faulting her work for becoming polemical, others have argued that her early poems also concerned the black experience and racial injustice. For example, *The Bean Eaters* (1960) includes protest poems about lynchings and segregation, and her first book, *A Street in Bronzeville* (1945), depicts African Americans struggling to get by in a place that has basically been abandoned by America. The critic Kenny Williams argues that in her work Brooks is able to "treat protest aesthetically without artistic compromise.... [H]er work transcends both region and race" (67).

Although the themes of her work may have remained consistent over the years, most critics, like Brooks herself, recognize the differences in the style and structure of her early work versus her later work. While most of her early poems are written in traditional forms, including sonnets, ballads, and Chaucerian stanzas, after 1967 Brooks began to experiment more heavily with free verse and the black vernacular. "I've written hundreds of sonnets. I feel, however, I'll never write another sonnet because it doesn't seem to me to be a sonnet kind of time," she claimed in 1984. "It seems to me to be a wild, raw, ragged, free-verse kind of time."

After her political "awakening," Brooks also began to think about audience in a way that she never had with her early work. "Much of that early work was addressed to blacks, but it happened without my conscious intention," she explained (Tate 40). After 1967, Brooks claimed that she wrote only for a black audience and, in fact, believed that white critics should be ignored. She felt that as a prominent poet, she could assist the development of Black Arts Movement. Although Brooks argued that she did not write poems "with the *idea* that they are to become 'social forces'" and felt that language itself was often the driving force of a poem, she also believed poems could lead to social change (Stravos 153). She did not want her poetry to only reach the ears of literary African Americans, but to be heard by those people who generally did not read poetry. She worked to compose poems that would be meaningful for this audience, and actively tried to bring poetry to the people, by reading in prisons, bars, and drug rehabilitation centers.

Gwendolyn Brooks underwent a life-changing experience at Fisk University, which affected her perspective, ideology, and poetry. Yet, regardless of how her work may have changed over the years, Brooks had always written about what she experienced and what she observed around her. No matter how her politics and beliefs transformed, the source of her poetry would never change. After all, poetry was not defined by politics, form, or language; instead, she remarked, "Poetry is life distilled" (interview 1984).

BEGINNINGS OF VERSE

Gwendolyn Elizabeth Brooks was born on June 17, 1917 to David and Keziah Brooks in Topeka, Kansas. A month after her birth, the family moved to Chicago. For all of her life, Brooks would consider Chicago her hometown.

Both of Brooks's parents, originally hailing from Kansas, lived in Chicago for most of their adult lives. Her father, David Anderson Brooks, born in Atchison, Kansas, was the son of a runaway field slave, Lucas Brooks. According to family legend, Lucas escaped from his slave master, then joined the Union Army during the Civil War. Lucas later married Elizabeth, a former house slave, and fathered twelve children.

When David was nine years old, his family, moving to rural Oklahoma and later Oklahoma City, struggled to survive hardship after hardship. Although food and money were scarce, David's parents often took in boarders and provided free meals to the hungry, an example of the generosity that David would later pass on to his own children. These early experiences and impressions shaped David's ambition and his perseverance. He encountered death at a young age, when two of his sisters died of pneumonia in the 1890s. When his father also died of the same illness, David became the primary caretaker for the family. Although none of his siblings had finished school, David was determined to graduate. In the mornings he would wake at five to feed the horses and complete all of the chores, and then he would walk to school.

After graduating from high school, David Brooks, believing in the possibility of the American dream, left behind the dust and destitution of Oklahoma to attend Fisk University, a black college in Nashville, Tennessee. David hoped to receive an education to prepare himself for medical school; however, the reality of the financial costs proved to be too daunting, and he dropped out of school after one year. Confident about finding work in a city, David Brooks then moved to Chicago in 1910, a year in which African Americans comprised 2% of the city's population, with the majority of the African-American workforce only able to obtain employment in the domestic and service sectors. David found work as a janitor for the McKinley Music Publishing Company, a job he would hold for thirty years.

During the summer of 1914, when he was thirty-one years old, David Brooks met Keziah Corine Wims, a fifth grade teacher in Topeka, Kansas, who had attended Emporia Normal, working as a maid to pay for her tuition. Although Keziah had always dreamed of becoming a concert pianist, the costs of training and schooling, and the lack of opportunities for African Americans, prompted her to abandon this hope. Instead, she turned to schooling and to the prospect of marriage. Two years after they met, David and Keziah were married in July 1916, at the home of Keziah's parents in Topeka.

The Brookses then moved to Chicago, but two and half months before the birth of their child, Keziah returned to Topeka to stay with her parents. After Gwendolyn was born on June 17, 1917, Keziah and her new daughter returned to Hyde Park, Chicago, to reunite with

David. Sixteen months after Gwendolyn's birth, Keziah gave birth to a son, Raymond.

The Brookses, endlessly searching for adequate and affordable housing, lived in several different residences throughout the city. Always hoping to buy a place of their own, David and Keziah found a modest house at 4332 South Champlain, located on Chicago's South Side, which would become their permanent residence. The neighborhood attracted David and Keziah for its safe streets, green lawns, large front porches, and peaceful atmosphere. Now that they were no longer confined to cramped apartment buildings, young Gwendolyn and Raymond could play freely in the yard, which also had a sandbox and hammock. When the Brookses moved in, they were the second African-American family on the block; eventually, the neighborhood would become a predominantly black neighborhood.

During the 1920s, more waves of migrations continued into the city, with African Americans and other ethnic communities settling into different neighborhoods. "[B]lack Chicago was as much a product of the American dream as other ethnic communities in the city," writes the critic Kenny Williams. "Despite failures and disappointments, there were many visible evidences of success" (53). For instance, there was a thriving black-owned business district, as well as impressive churches, various black-owned newspapers, and real estate firms. "With such a concentration of capital, people, and power, it is not surprising that the political organization of black Chicago was the envy of other cities," explains Williams (54). For new residents such as David and Keziah Brooks, and for the many African Americans looking to move to the city, Chicago offered opportunities and promises. However, over the years, economic pressures, racism, and housing shortages would devastate many of these dreams.

Despite economic hardships, the Brookses provided a stable environment for their children. Loving, supportive, and sometimes strict, Keziah and David read stories and sang songs to Gwendolyn and Raymond, already encouraging their creativity and intellectual pursuits at a young age. The atmosphere in the Brooks home was quiet and reserved, yet never dull. Both parents influenced Gwendolyn's love for reading and poetry. David Brooks often recited poems to his children, and both Gwendolyn and Raymond saw their father as a figure of kindness and power. He could build fires, paint the house, and fix anything that was broken, and yet he also sang, read, and played games with them. Her father's "kind eyes, song," his reverence for education, and his belief in persevering to overcome hardship, all impressed and shaped Gwendolyn's character (*Part One* 39). Her father made her feel safe and secure, and his generosity and tenderness were characteristics she hoped to emulate.

Whereas her father was more carefree and relaxed, Gwendolyn's "quick-walking, careful, Duty-loving mother" filled the house with a different kind of energy and peacefulness, encouraging creativity and yet also impressing upon Gwendolyn a respect for rules and propriety (*Part One* 39). Keziah was loving, but not usually demonstrative with hugs or kisses. She spent considerable time with her children, making them chocolate fudge, singing to them, or helping them with their homework. She fully believed in and encouraged her children's success. Active in the church, Keziah made sure that both children regularly attended Sunday School at the Carter Temple Church, located on the northwest corner of their block. The three attended without Gwendolyn's father, who had spent all of his life going to church but now made the choice not to attend. Keziah volunteered at the church to train a group of children in special musical programs, and she also began instructing Gwendolyn, at age four, to recite poetry, as Keziah admired people who could read with expression and enthusiasm. Thus, Gwendolyn, preschool-aged, often performed these poetry recitations in front of the congregation at church, her mother providing her with early training for the poetry readings that would become such a significant part of Gwendolyn's life.

Gwendolyn's aunts and uncles were also influential forces in the shaping of her childhood, with her mother's four sisters especially leaving lasting impressions on Gwendolyn. One aunt taught her to dance, while another delighted Gwendolyn with her sense of style, a "queen." Overall, Brooks experienced a happy childhood, one filled with songs, stories, radio programs, and games such as checkers and dominos. Holidays exemplified family warmth and intimacy, creating nostalgic memories of a brightly-lit tree, homemade fruitcake, and new books.

A quiet child, Brooks felt somewhat unprepared for the noisy, bustling atmosphere of elementary school. Although she liked the learning aspect of school, she found the social component of school perplexing and difficult. Early on, Gwendolyn felt that she did not fit in with the other children: "I had not brass or sass. I did not fight brilliantly, or at all, on the playground. I was not ingenious in gym, carrying my team single-handedly to glory. I could not play jacks. I could not ride a bicycle. I did not whisper excitedly about my Boyfriends" (*Part One* 38). The homemade dresses that her aunt Beulah sewed for her, her lack of athletic prowess, and her shy demeanor quickly set her apart from the popular children—who were generally from wealthier families, or light-skinned children with "good" hair. For the first time, Brooks encountered the politics of intraracial racism. Although Gwendolyn, dark-complexioned, had never been ashamed of her skin color—exclaiming, "*I* had always considered it beautiful. I would stick out my arm, examine it, and smile. Charming!"—she felt suddenly self-conscious and painfully aware of this color-caste system (*Part One* 39).

Brooks understandably felt more comfortable at home than at school. She often sat outside on the front porch, daydreaming and looking at the sky: "As a little girl I dreamed freely, often on the top step of the back porch—morning, moon, sunset, deep twilight" (*Part One* 55). She spent a great deal of time reading, eventually going through all of the Harvard Classics that lined her parents' bookshelf, including the work of Ralph Waldo Emerson, Hume, Locke, and Charles Darwin. She also knew the poetry of Paul Lawrence Dunbar, the well-known African-American poet of the late nineteenth century. Both Keziah and David encouraged their children to read, and as soon as Gwendolyn and Raymond were old enough, their mother signed them up for public library cards. Gwendolyn would check out four or five books at a time, read them as fast as she could, and then return them for more.

By age seven, Gwendolyn was writing two-line verses. She began filling up notebooks with her poems at age eleven. When her mother realized her aptitude for writing, she dismissed her from many of the household chores and encouraged her to write. Keziah proudly proclaimed, "You are going to be the *lady* Paul Lawrence Dunbar" (*Part One* 56).

Although in her autobiography Brooks focuses mostly on fond memories, her childhood was not an entirely idyllic time. When the stock market crashed in 1929, Gwendolyn was twelve years old, and the persisting and devastating effects of the Great Depression lasted throughout the 1930s and 1940s. Families all over the United States, including the Brookses, struggled to earn enough money to feed their children. Gwendolyn's father only earned twenty-five dollars a week, but during the lean years of the Depression, his wages dropped down to ten dollars. Keziah urged her husband to find a different job with better pay, but David felt he was fortunate to be employed at all, considering that so many were without work or homes. Throughout the 1930s, over half of the employable black population in Chicago was out of work, and 168,000 black families received government assistance (Kent 32). Gwendolyn's parents, though determined not to experience unemployment or to take government assistance, could not escape the growing anxiety and strain between them as they toiled to raise their children in these difficult times. Gwendolyn and her brother dreaded their parents' arguing. "[W]e would have been quite content to entertain a beany diet every day, if necessary," recalled Gwendolyn, adding, "if only there could be, continuously, the almost musical Peace that we had most of the time" (*Part One* 40). The strain and tension finally reached a point in which Keziah left for Topeka with Gwendolyn and Raymond. Then their father came for them, returning the children to Chicago, where they lived without their mother for a year. Although at the time young Gwendolyn felt abandoned by her mother, she chose later in life not to dwell on the way these particular events impacted her. Instead, as evident in her autobiography, she focused on how her parents and the mostly peaceful atmosphere of the house on 4332 South Champlain encouraged Gwendolyn to live her life with kindness and to follow her ambition.

Sweet Sixteen

When she was thirteen, Gwendolyn's father provided her with an old desk that McKinley's had given him, where she could now compose her poems. This was also the year she discovered *Writer's Digest*, a magazine with articles on writers' issues and obstacles; this "milestone" gave Brooks a sense of belonging to a new group that she had not realized existed (*Part One* 56). At this point, Brooks read mostly traditional European authors, such as Shakespeare, Wordsworth, Longfellow, Keats, Shelly, and Byron. The language and themes of these poets, and her daydreaming thoughts of God, angels, future lovers, and heroes, influenced much of her own youthful poetry. She filled up notebooks, writing a minimum of one poem per day. Also at age thirteen, she experienced the joy of seeing her work in print for the first time when her poem "Eventide" was published in the magazine *American Childhood*.

On the brink of adolescence, Brooks had not yet experienced love or relationships, but many of her poems during this time concerned themes of unrequited love: "I spent most of my free time in my room, writing, reading, reflecting. I was always mooning over some boy or other" (*Part One* 57). She also fed into her dreamy notions of love by avidly watching films—those love stories that starred Clara Bow, Bette Davis, Clark Gable, Spencer Tracy, or Katherine Hepburn. All of her screen heroes were white, as African Americans did not often appear in movies, except to fill minor roles, which typically were racist representations, depicting the characters as ignorant, lazy, or savage. Brooks later recalled, "Secretly we were ashamed of those Black folks up there: we felt their love for money exceeded their pride" (*Part Two* 17).

Although she had made several friends, Brooks preferred spending her time alone. She felt like the other kids found her strange because she always wanted to be in her room writing: "I had friends, but I felt alone inside" (Lewis 170). Brooks, who was quite shy, felt awkward and timid at parties, where her peers often danced or played Post Office, a kissing game in which the girls would receive a "letter" from a boy. Brooks rarely received "letters"; nor was she asked to dance. She admitted her inexperience and her tendency to withdrawal from these social situations: "At the age of fourteen I was fonder of paper dolls than of parties" (*Part One* 57). In the presence of the more popular children, Brooks continued to feel self-conscious about her physical appearance and also of her shyness: "I was timid to the point of terror, silent, primly dressed. AND DARK" (57).

As she moved into adolescence, her relationship with her mother grew more complex and difficult, and Gwendolyn began to inwardly rebel against her mother's strictness, questioning the importance Keziah placed on decency and rectitude. Poetry seemed to be Brooks's only escape from her mother's rules and from the perplexing social web at school, which placed emphasized popularity, prettiness, and athletic ability. Brooks changed high schools several times. First, she attended Hyde Park Branch School, one of the leading, and predominately white, public schools in Chicago. She had not been around many white children in her life time, and suddenly she now was swept into a school where the white students basically ignored the existence of the black students: "I realized they were a society apart, and they really made you feel it" (Lewis 172). Brooks then transferred to an all-back high school, Wendell Phillips, hoping to feel more accepted and comfortable. However, at Wendell Phillips, Brooks encountered more intolerance, which again seemed based on the darkness of her skin, as well as her shyness. She did not know the latest dances (she only knew the Charleston, which her aunt had taught her), she wore homemade dresses, and she did not possess the confidence of the popular girls: "I just slumped through the halls, quiet, hugging my books" (Lewis 172).

She transferred this time to Englewood, an integrated school, where she found it easier to make friends. However, she still did not date boys, nor was she popular. One story from her adolescence in particular reveals her loneliness. She had decided to give a party for her sixteenth birthday, with her mother and aunts helping her with decorations and refreshments. She then waited all afternoon, to no avail, for her peers to show up; Brooks was left to celebrate her Sweet Sixteen with mostly members of her own family.

However, something else occurred during her sixteenth year that would end up being far more meaningful than any Sweet Sixteen party. In his biography of Brooks, George Kent attests, "The triumph of her sixteenth year was not to be social or coming to terms with boys: it was to be in her writing and the communications she had with black writer James Weldon Johnson" (26). When she was sixteen, Brooks sent James Weldon Johnson, a civil rights leader and a prominent writer of the Harlem Renaissance, several of her poems. To her delight, Johnson responded with a letter of encouragement and praise. He said that she obviously possessed talent, but also suggested that she read modern poets. Acting on his advice, Brooks turned to poets such as T.S. Eliot, Ezra Pound, and E.E. Cummings. The poet Emily Dickenson also influenced her work.

Gwendolyn Brooks then had the rare opportunity to meet James Weldon Johnson in person when he spoke at a neighboring church. Gwendolyn's mother escorted Gwendolyn to the church; and, after Johnson's talk, encouraged her daughter to approach him. Brooks found the austere Johnson to be distant and aloof, and when she was too intimidated to speak up, Keziah interrupted and reminded him that he had mailed her daughter a letter of encouragement. James Weldon Johnson could not recall Brooks's name or her poetry. When he explained that he dealt with a multitude of young artists, both Gwendolyn and her mother felt snubbed.

On the other hand, not long after meeting Johnson, Brooks had the opportunity to hear the famous Harlem Renaissance poet Langston Hughes speak at the Metropolitan Community Church. Brooks was already quite familiar with and impressed by Hughes's poetry. She had read Countee Cullen's anthology of black writers, *Caroling Dusk*, where she had encountered the work of Langston Hughes and other Harlem Renaissance authors.

Her mother again escorted her, with a stack of her daughter's poems in hand. When Gwendolyn and Keziah approached Hughes, he responded with warmth and friendliness. At Keziah's request, he read Gwendolyn's poems on the spot, and then told Gwendolyn that she was "talented and must go on writing" (Lewis 174). Later, during Brooks's adult years, she would stay in close touch with Hughes.

Before these notable interactions with established writers, Brooks had felt like she had no one to talk to about writing, except for her family. Now she had the encouragement of two Harlem Renaissance authors, as well as support from a few of the teachers at Englewood who were beginning to notice her talent for writing. For example, to the surprise of an English teacher, Brooks once turned in a book report constructed entirely in rhyme. At a young age, Brooks was a disciplined and prolific writer, once listing as her New Year's resolution to "write some poetry everyday" (Kent 27). She already considered herself a poet, but now that she had outside endorsement, she felt others were also taking her seriously. When she was sixteen, she began publishing her poems in the *Chicago Defender*, a black newspaper, and in two years, the newspaper had published seventy-five of her poems.

FINDING WORK

The effects of the Depression severely hit Chicago's black neighborhoods. It was difficult for African Americans to find housing, with the majority of the black population crowded into the South Side, where buildings and homes had been allotted to bring the most money for the least amount of space. The urban occurrence of "white flight" had been happening for years, with the Brooks's neighborhood by now transforming into an all-black neighborhood. Lack of employment and housing contributed to a sense of despair. "By the 1930s and 1940s, the heirs to the American dream had become the disenchanted and the dispossessed," asserts Williams (55).

Gwendolyn's parents struggled to make ends meet, with her father now working part-time painting stores and apartments at night, in addition to his full-time job as a janitor. Her brother also worked part-time, while Gwendolyn helped her mother, taking on more of the household chores. Often their meals consisted only of beans. Although at first, college seemed like an impossibility, a new two-year city college, Wilson Junior College, opened in the fall after Brooks's high school graduation. Wilson offered an affordable education, charging approximately six dollars per semester. Despite the financially difficult times, Gwendolyn's parents supported her decision to continue her education after high school. After graduating from high school in 1934, Brooks attended Wilson, majoring in English.

Brooks graduated from the two-year college in 1936 at age nineteen. Now she would be facing the effects of the Great Depression on a more personal level, as she too now had to look for a job. Since she had published many poems in the *Chicago Defender*, Brooks hoped that the newspaper would hire her as a reporter. She wrote to Robert S. Abbott, the well-respected African-American publisher, and Abbott responded cordially, asking her to come in for an interview. Keziah accompanied Gwendolyn to Abbott's office. According to both mother and daughter, once Abbott saw Gwendolyn, his attitude immediately changed, and he became indifferent, even unfriendly. According to her biographer, Brooks suspected that Abbott had denied her the job because of her dark skin (Kent 41). Although discouraged, Brooks was not defeated. She had been facing issues of racism and intraracial tensions since she was a child, and these early experiences had contributed to her racial pride and self-confidence. Brooks had never felt ashamed of her skin color, but rather ashamed that others, both black and white, were so narrow-minded and prejudiced. A year before, Brooks had coined a poem of outrage and protest concerning a job application in which a black woman had written: "I've Negroid features, but they're finely spaced" (Kent 36). Brooks had always reacted strongly toward blacks attempting to measure themselves with white standards of beauty. Many years later she would write a poem praising black women who did not straighten their hair, "To Those of my Sisters Who Kept Their Naturals" (1980).

Abbott never called her back about the job and Brooks, for her own gratification, published her own mimeographed newspaper, which featured poetry, local politics, and editorials. However, a self-published newspaper would not pay the bills. Brooks finally joined the domestic work force, practically the only opportunity for an African-American woman, and worked as a cleaning woman and maid. After those jobs, which she felt were humiliating and degrading, she then spent four months working for a "spiritual adviser" who sold potions and charms to the residents of the Mecca Building, a dilapidated and sprawling tenement building on Chicago's South Side. The advisor would send Brooks and his other assistants through the Mecca to sell love charms and other trinkets to the poor and weary, and in Brooks's opinion, this was her most reprehensible job. Although she earned eight dollars a week, a quarter of which she gave to her parents, she felt relieved when she was fired for not taking a promotion, which would have required her to preach.

In addition to working, Brooks continued to make time in her day to write, composing poems not only about unrequited love, but also racial pride. Her work was beginning to receive more recognition, with poems appearing in two different anthologies. When she was twenty years old, four years after she sent her early poems to James Weldon Johnson, she mailed him several of her newest poems, and he replied once again with encouragement and specific criticism. Although he especially liked her poem "Reunion," which was published in the journal *Crisis* in 1937, he also pointed out her problems, what he considered to be sentimental diction and awkward lines. "Don't be afraid to put in an extra syllable," he suggested (Kent 27).

Then, at the suggestion of a friend, Brooks attended a meeting of the local National Association of the Advancement of Colored People Youth Council. Unlike high school, the ambitious young men and women at the NAACP accepted and welcomed her: "Gwendolyn found herself immediately accepted as a valuable addition—someone who had definite skills to offer, and, on those occasions when she spoke, something to say" (Kent 43). The NAACP Youth Council provided her with stimulating company. She became friends with Margaret Taylor Burroughs, who would become a well-known painter, and the two would remain friendly for years. Engaged with the dynamics of this group, Brooks became more involved, and in 1937, she accepted the position as publicity director. On a political and civic level, she found herself growing more aware of social injustices, and participating in marches and protests.

For the first time, Brooks had a large group of friends. She also began dating. The dates usually consisted of taking long walks, or sitting together on her parents' front porch. Then one day, before a Youth Council meeting, she was standing outside the YWCA building when she saw Henry Lowington Blakely II, also an aspiring poet. The twenty-one year old Brooks took one look at him and said to Margaret, "There is the man I am going to marry." Immediately, Margaret called out, "Hey, boy, this girl wants to meet you!" (*Part One* 58).

LIVING IN KITCHENETTES

Two years later Gwendolyn and Henry were married. The simple ceremony took place on September 17, 1939, in Gwendolyn's parents' living room, and was attended by close friends and family. It was Gwendolyn's mother, not her father, who spoke up when the minister asked who gave Gwendolyn and Henry away in marriage. Both of her parents approved of the marriage, but Henry's mother, Pearl, felt more hesitant about the union; she considered her son to be too naïve and whimsical to be a husband, and she worried he was unprepared to find a job. Henry descended from a family much different from Gwendolyn's. He had grown up quite poor, and spent much of his young life moving around. After his father had abandoned the family when Henry was thirteen, he had been raised single-handedly by his mother.

Gwendolyn expressed no doubts about her new husband, describing him as "a man of intellect, imagination" (*Part One* 58). Gwendolyn and Henry were determined to follow their dreams to be poets, and they faced the grim reality of finding work and a home with youthful exuberance. Although the prospect of a young black couple finding good jobs and affordable housing was nearly impossible in a racially and class-divided 1940s Chicago, Gwendolyn and Henry remained hopeful: "In facing the raw economics and brutally discriminatory housing of Chicago, Gwendolyn and Henry had naturally a certain innocence, optimism, and youth as their capital" (Kent 52).

During WWII, 60,000 African Americans migrated into the city, increasing the pressure to find affordable housing (Kent 52). Gwendolyn and Henry moved through a series of dingy, cramped apartments. Their first apartment was a small, drab kitchenette in the Tyson Apartments at 43rd and South Park. In her autobiography, Brooks describes the reality of the poverty that was tempered by their joyfulness: "It is not true that the poor are never "happy." ... [E]ven in the cramped dreariness of the Tyson there was fun, there was company, there was reading, mutual reading" (59). As Henry and Gwendolyn moved again and again, each time to dismal kitchenettes or small apartments without private bathrooms, these real-life experiences became the subject matter of Gwendolyn's work. One of her most well-known early poems, "kitchenette," concerns those cramped, often depressing living quarters.

In addition to the housing shortage, the employment opportunities for African Americans were restricted to mostly unskilled and semi-skilled labor, with the sectors such as public utilities, electrical, manufacturing, banks, and offices holding a whites-only employment policy. After a long search, Henry found a job working for a black insurance company, but the money and hours proved to be unstable. Despite the financial strains, Henry and Gwendolyn continued to place a high priority on intellectual and artistic pursuits, while Henry's mother and other family members "were most concerned about the amount of time Gwendolyn and Henry gave to poetry while they were facing one of the toughest and most discriminatory labor markets in the country" (Kent 53). Gwendolyn remained dedicated to composing poems, regardless of recognition or reward: "Indeed, one who chooses to become a poet does well not to think of money or even of making a living by the writing of verse. I wrote because I wanted to. I knew I'd always compose poetry, whether it was published or not" (Angle 131). Henry supported Gwendolyn's ambition, reading and responding to her work with helpful criticism and encouragement. However, as Henry spent more time in the workforce, trying to earn wages to pay their rent and bills, he obviously had less time to compose his own poetry.

By 1939, Gwendolyn's work was becoming less influenced by the poetry of the European masters, and more influenced by the changing world around her, as black artistic communities, closely intertwined with Leftist social ideals, were beginning expand and influence the city. A particularly important group that began in 1936 was the South Side Writers Group, organized by the novelist Richard Wright. Although Gwendolyn was not a member of the group, she was friends with people who were, including Margaret Walker, a poet and novelist, Ted Ward, a playwright, and Edward Bland, a poet and critic. These writers influenced and engaged Gwendolyn with their work and their social ideas. While Walker and Ward were more radical, fusing politics and art, Bland, according to Kent, held a "simpler humanistic point of view" and took interest in "the interaction between social forces and literature" (55). As she met more writers and artists, Brooks's conservative, middle-class, Christian upbringing was often at odds with the ideas she was now encountering. Although the changes in her own opinions and politics were subtle, as she interacted with more black artists and writers, she began to question certain "absolute" values and to examine closely the sources of her poetry. Kent suggests that Gwendolyn's "experiences were so distant from the idyllic ones of her parental home that she had to develop more ways of seeing the world. Her new sensibility would respond more rapidly to artistic possibilities and to the social world of artists" (59).

A more personal transformation occurred on October 10, 1940, when Gwendolyn gave birth to her son, Henry Jr. The addition to the family drastically changed Gwendolyn and Henry's routine, and also increased financial pressure. They moved from apartment to apartment, searching for something decent and affordable. In terms of housing and finances, the outlook appeared bleak. Sometimes to escape and to find temporary relief, Henry and Gwendolyn went to the movies, which usually cheered them up. However, on their way home from seeing *The Wizard of Oz*, Gwendolyn began to cry, perhaps overwhelmed by the fantastical magnificence of Oz and its juxtaposition to the shabby, depressing environment in which they lived (Kent 58). The trouble with money began to affect their happy marriage and positive outlook, with tensions escalating until one decisive day when Henry angrily threw a firecracker in Gwendolyn and Henry Jr.'s direction. Gwendolyn immediately left him and went to her parents with her son, vowing never to return. But after her parents urged a reconciliation, she went back to him. Slowly, their lives began to stabilize. Henry changed jobs to work in the Defense Department, and then the family moved into a small second-floor apartment on East 63rd Street, where they would stay for seven years.

POETRY WORKSHOP AND PUBLICATIONS

In 1941, a poetry class for black writers started at Chicago's South Side Community Art Center. The instructor of the class was Inez Cunningham Stark, a wealthy white socialite from the city's "Gold Coast." An aristocratic writer and scholar, Stark hoped to cultivate the talents of aspiring black poets. In her autobiography, Brooks characterizes Stark as a "rebel," to her class and race, whose white friends feared she would be killed or raped by the African-American students. Gwendolyn recalled Stark's notable entrance into the classroom: "tripping in, slender, erect, and frosted with a fabulous John Frederick's hat[,] ... [h]er arms would be loaded with books" (*Part One* 66).

Both Gwendolyn and Henry, twenty-four years old, enrolled in the classes, which would be quite valuable in developing Gwendolyn's craft and talents; during this time, her poetry underwent a significant maturation and evolution. As Brooks expanded her knowledge of contemporary poets, she also took Stark's advice to write about personal experiences, and the poems she wrote during the class depicted an urban realism. Brooks soon realized that despite her small apartment on 63rd Street, the area invited poetry: "If you wanted a poem, you had only to look out of a window. There was material always, walking or running, fighting or screaming or singing" (*Part One* 69). What she saw all around her was a mix of poverty and creativity, from cramped kitchenettes to blues and jazz. "These raw, realistic, no-nonsense confrontations," observes Kent, "combined with the thin stream of contacts from the Chicago Black Renaissance of the 1930s to push Gwendolyn's artistic sensibility further toward sophistication and poetic realism" (53). For the rest of her career, Gwendolyn would write poems about what she saw around her. She believed that "any of the materials of life are the proper materials for poetry" (interview 1984).

On the reading board for the renowned magazine *Poetry*, Stark encouraged the participants to read prominent poets, gave prosodic instruction, and led the class in workshops. The students critiqued their own work, as well as the work of published authors, and they spoke frankly, often ripping apart the poems and stinging each other with their criticisms. "We were encouraged to tear each other to pieces," Brooks recalled (Lewis 174). While the students were often passionate and uproarious, Stark's own opinions were delivered in a different manner— "cool, objective, frank" (*Part One* 66). Brooks learned much about language, form, and audience from Stark, and credited her with teaching her "to fear the cliché" (Angle 139). Furthermore, the classes gave Gwendolyn the rare opportunity to be around other serious black artists, writers, and intellectuals, including Edward Bland, William Couch, John Carlis, Margaret Taylor Burroughs, and Margaret Danner, who would all go on to become critics, poets, and artists. The energetic dynamic in the class inspired Brooks: "How serious we were, how enchanted with each other and with ourselves! How diligently we learned and taught each other" (*Part One* 67).

Yet as Gwendolyn expresses in her autobiography, "Poetry was not the whole of life" (*Part One* 68). The years of 1941–49 were also a period rich with social events and parties that included both white and black guests, many of them well known, such as the performer/activist Paul Robeson or the poet Margaret Walker. At this point, Gwendolyn knew most of the black writers and artists living in Chicago, and the energy of this community, as well as the city's vibrant blues scene and politics, influenced her poetic sensibilities. She cultivated many relationships with prominent black writers and artists, including her mentor, Langston Hughes. Gwendolyn and Henry once threw a party at their place on 63rd Street for Hughes. Seventy-five friends packed into their tiny apartment, and Hughes "enjoyed everyone; he enjoyed all the talk, all the phonograph blues, all the festivity in the crowded air" (*Part One* 70). Gwendolyn admired Hughes for the way he reached out to the younger poets and encouraged them in their work, and felt grateful for the support he gave to her. He would later devote several of his newspaper columns to praising Brooks's poetry, and he also dedicated his book of short stories, *Something in Common*, to her.

Not only did Inez Cunningham Stark encourage her students to read poetry and challenge them with language and form, she also pushed them to enter writing competitions. This advice paid off for Brooks in 1943, when she won a poetry award from the Midwestern Writers Conference. Soon after, an editor for Knopf, Emily Morison, congratulated her and asked to see her poems. Gwendolyn sent about forty of her poems, most of them dealing with "universal" themes of abstractions such as love and war, and Morison wrote back and said she liked the "Negro" poems best. She requested that Gwendolyn approach Knopf again when she had more of these. Fearing another rejection from Knopf, Gwendolyn instead sent the batch of poems, along with new ones, to the publishing house Harper & Brothers.

The Harper editor Elizabeth Lawrence contacted Gwendolyn with the announcement that Harper would publish the book, and she encouraged Brooks to take a year or two to write the rest of the poems. Determined for the book to be published soon, Gwendolyn worked feverishly to compose the rest of the poems, cutting parties, movies, and other social events out of her life. She did not work under idyllic, peaceful conditions—Gwendolyn always managed to combine real-life work with her writing. With her son now almost four years old, he needed much attention and care, and Gwendolyn found herself trying to write while "[s]crubbing, sweeping, washing, ironing, cooking: dropping the mop, broom, soap, iron, or carrot grater to write down a line, or word" (Kent 64).

The support of the Harper editor Elizabeth Lawrence was undoubtedly important for Gwendolyn Brooks's career. The two would develop a long, close working relationship, which Kent describes as "somewhat maternal, since Elizabeth Lawrence was the older and more worldly" (65). The first time they met, Gwendolyn felt nervous and shy around this white woman. However, she soon found herself talking to Lawrence about the craft of poetry, literary technique, and her own views on her role as a black writer. Brooks, reacting against the Harlem Renaissance period in which often a white audience was drawn to the "exotica" of black people, felt confident that her poetry portrayed African Americans as ordinary people: "It is my privilege to state Negroes not as curios but as people" (Angle 146).

Not only did she have the support of Elizabeth Lawrence, Gwendolyn also had a letter of encouragement from the African-American novelist Richard Wright, to whom Harper had sent the poems for his evaluation. Wright had reacted positively to the work. Although he criticized some of the poems, overall he felt they were successful, claiming, "Miss Brooks is real and so are her poems" (Kent 62). Gwendolyn, an admirer of Wright's novels, wrote him back two letters of appreciation.

Before Gwendolyn's book was published, she received more exposure with publications and prizes. Several of her poems were published in *Poetry*, *Common Ground*, and *Negro Story*, and she also won another Midwestern Writers Conference prize in 1945. Then, to her delight, *A Street in Bronzeville* appeared in the bookstores on August 15, 1945. Gwendolyn had received ten copies of the slim book a couple of weeks before the release date: "I took out the first copy. I tuned the pages of the thin little thing, over and over. My Book" (*Part One* 72).

In the first part of *A Street in Bronzeville*, the poems document the everyday lives of and disappointments of African Americans living in Bronzeville, or the "South Side Black Belt"—the crowded black neighborhood which had begun to deteriorate over the years, with the construction of giant public housing complexes swallowing up private homes and lack of economic support sending the neighborhood into ruin. In her poems, Brooks gives these dispossessed, forgotten inhabitants of Chicago a chance to speak. "This is not the Chicago of the elite, not the city of spectacular boulevards and buildings," Williams says of Brooks's depiction of Bronzeville. "This is a city of backstreets and alleys, of kitchenettes and vacant lots" (55). The second half of the book details the unfair treatment of African Americans in the military during WWII.

A Street in Bronzeville received much critical acclaim, and Brooks was praised as a major new voice in contemporary poetry. The Chicago critic Paul Engle, who had recently presented Gwendolyn with the 1945 Midwestern Writers Conference Award for poetry, had told Gwendolyn that his review would appear in the *Chicago Tribune*. On the way home from a movie, Gwendolyn and Henry purchased the Sunday edition and then stopped under a streetlight to read one of the first reviews of the book. Brooks felt that Engle's positive review "was the review that initiated My Reputation!" (*Part One* 72) The success of *Bronzeville* quickly led to more success. Shortly after its publication, Brooks received her first Guggenheim award, and was also named one of the "Ten Women of the Year" by *Mademoiselle* magazine.

CRITICAL SUCCESS

Gwendolyn's career started anspiciously. The publication of *Bronzeville* began to establish her reputation and give her more prominence within the literary world. These years were exciting and productive, not only in terms of Gwendolyn's career, but also in regard to her social world. Gwendolyn and Henry knew many famous painters, poets, dancers, actors, and photographers. The numerous parties, which included everything from the fabulous, costly parties at Evelyn Gann's three-story house, to long discussions over drinks and food in crowded apartments, provided Gwendolyn with many new friendships and connections to the art and literary world.

When she was thirty-one, Gwendolyn began to write book reviews for poetry and novels, expanding her career as a poet to include that of a respected critic. Gwendolyn's reviews were notable for their straightforward, direct approach. She liked to say that at this period in her life, she had "sturdy ideas about writing" (*Part One* 72). Over the span of fifteen years she would review for such publications as the *Chicago Daily News*, the *Chicago Sun-Times*, the *Chicago Tribune*, *Negro Digest*, the *New York Times*, and the *New York Herald Tribune*.

As she met new authors and critics, Gwendolyn also cultivated her relationship with her editor, Elizabeth Lawrence. Elizabeth was supportive and encouraging of Gwendolyn from the start. She also provided Gwendolyn with trustworthy and insightful criticism and praise. In March 1948, Gwendolyn sent Elizabeth a group of poems she wanted to include in a new collection. While Elizabeth felt excited about the poems, believing that Brooks was "undoubtedly in the process of evolving a new style," she also realized they needed to be improved (Kent 76). To get an outside opinion, Elizabeth sent the manuscript to the poet Genevieve Taggard, who responded with eight hand-written pages of predominately negative criticism, citing obscurity, ungraspable diction, and lack of development as major weaknesses. Feeling that some of Taggard's comments and criticisms would be helpful to Gwendolyn, Elizabeth sent the response to Brooks, along with a letter of support and a contract to publish the book.

In her letter, Elizabeth assured Gwendolyn, "As I am sure you know, I regard you as a writer of rare talent and an authentic poet.... It seems to me that this present collection shows you in transition.... You are too good a poet to have to resort to tricks and shock devices" (Kent 77). Gwendolyn expressed gratitude for the contract, although the advance on royalties for $100 was only half of what she received for her first book. Her reaction to Taggard's views was reasonably mixed. Although Brooks felt some of the criticism was valid, she also felt Taggard was wrong in many instances, and she vigorously defended her work to Elizabeth. She acknowledged that Elizabeth was correct about her searching for a new style, and consented to a few of the changes. After revising these poems and writing a group of new poems, Gwendolyn sent the completed manuscript back to Elizabeth in January 1949.

Annie Allen appeared in the summer of 1949 to mostly positive reviews, although a few critics cited "obscurity" as a problem. The poems in *Annie Allen*, many of them sonnets that experiment with both conventional and unconventional structures, chronicle the story of a black woman's journey from childhood to adulthood.

With the publication of *Annie Allen*, Brooks began to acquire more success and public recognition. A five-page favorable review by the poet Stanley Kunitz appeared in the literary journal *Poetry*, which also published several of Brooks's poems and awarded her its Eunice Tietjens Memorial Prize. Langston Hughes praised Gwendolyn in his new magazine, *Voices*: "The people and the poems in Gwendolyn Brooks' book are alive, reaching, and very much of today" (5). A radio station aired a play, called *Poet in Bronzeville*, that attempted to portray Gwendolyn's life. Although the drama contained several errors, Brooks felt pleased with it overall, believing that it depicted her as a poet who belonged to the people rather than to critics and other poets. As Gwendolyn continued to receive public exposure, she attended autograph parties and made various public appearances, including a reading at the predominately black college Howard University.

Despite all of the positive response toward her work, Gwendolyn was struggling to overcome financial troubles. She applied for a John Hay Whitney Fellowship with a recommendation from her editor, but she did not win. Then, in 1950, her career was suddenly invigorated by a tremendous honor: the Pulitzer Prize. Gwendolyn, winning the award for *Annie Allen*, became the first African American, in any genre, to win a Pulitzer Prize. She was thirty-three years old.

Suddenly her fairly quiet life was overwhelmed by phone calls, fan mail, and invitations. People sent their poetry manuscripts, hoping for a supportive response, and several people even dropped by her apartment, wanting to catch a glimpse of her. Although at this point she declined the many offers for interviews, feeling too shy, Gwendolyn did attend readings, parties, and other various social events.

Now that she had more public obligations, she found herself struggling to find time to write. While Henry worked for an automobile business, Gwendolyn tried to write poetry in the mornings until her son came home from school. To supplement her income, she wrote book reviews. Despite the prestige of winning the Pulitzer, money still seemed scarce and elusive. At one point, to ease the financial burden, Henry,

Gwendolyn, and Henry Jr. shared an apartment with Henry's work partner; however, Gwendolyn found it impossible to concentrate or to feel comfortable in this temporary housing situation. Out of desperation, Gwendolyn left with her son to Kalamazoo, Michigan, where she and Henry owned a house that they had purchased in order to rent to tenants. Soon Gwendolyn missed her home city, and she and her son returned to Chicago. While Henry slept in the downtown garage he helped to manage, Gwendolyn and Henry Jr. moved into an apartment in a rough neighborhood on South Evans. Finally, after living in several apartments, in April 1951, the family moved to an apartment on West 17th Street, paying $100 per month.

The shortage in adequate housing was not a problem unique to Gwendolyn and Henry. At the end of WWII, employment and housing discrimination against African Americans increased, creating racial conflicts throughout the city. Between 1940 and 1950, reports Kent, the black population increased from 277,731 to 492,265, yet Chicago refused to extend the area to which the black population was basically confined, and between 1945 and 1954, at least nine major race riots occurred in Chicago, with housing the major cause of conflict (94). One of Brooks's most directly political essays during this time, "They Call it Bronzeville," concerns the housing problem. Published in *Holiday* in 1951, the essay reveals Gwendolyn's growing awareness of the institutionalized racism around her, despite the popular optimistic attitudes of this post-WWII era.

For the most part, Gwendolyn embraced the popular WWII optimism that promised that times were changing and soon the country would be better for all Americans, including African Americans, who would soon obtain full equality and freedom. A popular point of view among black and white intellectuals during this optimistic period, explains George Kent, was that writers should aim to be universal and global with their subjects and themes. When *Phylon*, Atlanta University's scholarly journal, ran a special issue, "The Negro in Literature: The Current Scene," to debate this issue, Gwendolyn contributed an essay called "Poets Who Are Negroes." The essay focuses on the craft of writing poetry, and for the most part, steers away from directly addressing political and social concerns. It is interesting that many of the other essayists in the journal, points out Kent, recognized Gwendolyn as an example of "a new wave of emancipated black writers" who were more concerned with "form and craft" and "exploration of non-racial themes, and global thinking" than they were issues of race (98).

POET TURNED NOVELIST

In early 1951, Gwendolyn, thirty-four years old, was pregnant again. During her pregnancy, she worked mainly on book reviews and articles. The committee for the National Book Award invited her to be a judge, and she made a trip to New York City for the selection of the award. Then on September 8, 1951, her daughter, Nora, was born.

Now with two children (Henry, Jr. was now eleven years old), Gwendolyn felt determined to settle into a permanent home. She had spent most of her adult life on the move, and she was tired of the constant upheaval and the confining spaces. Gwendolyn and Henry began looking for a home, facing the problem of the housing shortage and lack of finances, and Gwendolyn, assuming that prose would be more salable than poetry, began to invest her energy in writing fiction.

Gwendolyn had submitted a version of a book of prose in 1945, then under the title "American Family Brown," to the Guggenheim Foundation, which awarded her a Fellowship, and to Harper, which did not offer her a contract. While praising Gwendolyn's characterizations, Elizabeth had expressed concern about her handling of dramatic conflict. Over the years, the manuscript had gone through extensive transformations, and Gwendolyn and Elizabeth had exchanged many opinions and ideas about the book. When Gwendolyn sent Elizabeth a new version of the manuscript, now calling the collection of short stories "Bronzevillians" in January 1952, Elizabeth found the idea interesting, but returned the manuscript again for more work. Gwendolyn revised the manuscript several more times, and realized during the process that instead of short stories, the book should be told in the form of a novel about a single character, Maud Martha. Ten months after Elizabeth's initial response, Gwendolyn sent the revised manuscript to her again, and this time Elizabeth offered her a contract and a $500 advance against royalties. Although enthusiastic about the novel, Elizabeth also pushed Gwendolyn to improve the manuscript. For example, she wanted Gwendolyn to more closely examine the marriage in the book, to develop the relationship between Maud Martha and her husband.

Gwendolyn and Elizabeth continued to exchange ideas and opinions about the work, securing their close relationship as editor and writer. Then, almost a year after Gwendolyn had sent Elizabeth the draft of "Bronzevillians," she sent her what she hoped was the final version, with a detailed letter describing her revisions. Elizabeth enthusiastically endorsed the work, and presented only a few more suggestions, one concerning the title—Harper wanted to call it "Daughter of the Dusk."

Gwendolyn disagreed with the publisher's title, but she felt relieved that the revisions were finished. Now she focused on the publicity and monetary potential of the book. She sent chapters of the novel to magazines, including *Life, Ebony, Harper's Bazaar,* and *Mademoiselle*, in hopes of earning payments and widening her audience. Elizabeth warned Gwendolyn not to be too hopeful about the book's earnings, reminding her that successful literature often does not equal financial success. To Gwendolyn's disappointment, none of the magazines accepted the submissions.

Eventually, Gwendolyn and Henry managed to sell the Michigan rental house. With the money from the sale, and after borrowing money from Gwendolyn's parents and their friends, they realized they had enough money to purchase a small, modest house on South Evans. Unfortunately, the publication of *Maud Martha* (the final title pleasing both author and publisher) did not bring in great sums of money; however, the novel did garner more publicity and critical prestige for Gwendolyn.

Comprising thirty-four short chapters, and totaling 180 pages, *Maud Martha* was published in September 1953 and received many supportive reviews from renowned newspapers, including the *Chicago Tribune*, the *New York Times*, the *Chicago Daily News*, and the *Chicago Sun-Times*. Partly an autobiographical novel, *Maud Martha* concerns the life of an African-American woman living in the WWII-era, and portrays the racism, sexism, and classism she encounters by both whites and blacks.

Although Elizabeth felt happy for Gwendolyn, she also felt the book had not been worked to its full potential, and exchanged comments about the novel with Gwendolyn's early mentor, Inez Stark Boulton (her name after marriage). Elizabeth honestly felt that the critics had been too gentle with Gwendolyn, although she hoped the support would bolster Gwendolyn's confidence to write a better book. Elizabeth wanted

Gwendolyn to push herself, to write outside of her own self and try different perspectives. Unlike Elizabeth's, Inez's criticisms were not literary, but more focused on politics—she felt the book was too segregated: "We are at the turning point, don't you think, where racial segregation should not be stressed, since so many advantages have been accorded Negroes in the last two years" (Kent 113). She asked that Elizabeth not show her comments to Gwendolyn. The exchange of letters between these two white women emphasizes the complexity of black artist relationships with well-meaning white liberals, points out Kent, and reveals the often patronizing tone that accompanied support: "[Inez's] letter expresses a concept that so frequently infuriated blacks: two enlightened whites conspiring to put a well-meaning but somewhat benighted black in line" (113). Gwendolyn's relationship with Inez was already complicated by an earlier incident, when the two had been in New York City in 1949. They had stopped by the Barbizon Plaza Hotel, where Inez was staying and where Gwendolyn wanted to stop in to change her clothes, but the hotel clerk would not allow Gwendolyn to go up to the room. When Inez casually remarked that perhaps she should have refused to stay there, as a matter of principle, Gwendolyn felt that she did not really take the matter seriously (Kent 88). Later in her life, Gwendolyn would become more ambivalent about support from the white literary establishment: although she was appreciative of the immense endorsement, she also questioned if African-American artists and white supporters could ever be on an equal footing.

In October, a month after the publication of *Maud Martha*, Gwendolyn's family moved into the new house on Chicago's South Side. Although Gwendolyn felt satisfied to finally be able to establish roots, the lack of money, as usual, threatened to consume her happiness. Gwendolyn's work was receiving international recognition, including the translation of a poem into Serbian, and a set of poems to be included in a German anthology, but she was not earning large sums of money. Hopeful, she applied for a teaching position at Roosevelt University, but was subsequently turned down for the job.

After the critical success of *Maud Martha*, Gwendolyn considered writing more books of prose. She had an idea for another novel about a character called Lincoln West. However, after being contacted by the children's division of Harper, she soon put the novel aside to spend time writing children's poems. After writing one poem per day, Gwendolyn had enough for a book called *Bronzeville Boys and Girls*. Most of the positive reviews focused on the "universal" appeal of the book, stressing that the book was not only directed toward black children. Ironically, the illustrator for the book gave all of the children white faces, something Gwendolyn found disturbing, but she did not protest.

RETURN TO POETRY

In the 1950s, racial tensions, violence, and injustices were slowly building toward the culmination and victory of the Civil Rights Movement. On May 17, 1954, in *Brown vs. Board of Education*, the Supreme Court's historic decision against school segregation gave the Civil Rights Movement a new wave of energy and impetus. However, there was also much backlash and violence, especially across the South. One of these incidents hit close to home. A year after the Supreme Court's decision, in the summer of 1955, Emmett Till, a fourteen-year-old from Chicago visiting relatives in Mississippi, was beaten, slain, and dumped in the river because he supposedly made advances to a white woman; the two accused white men were acquitted.

During these turbulent times, Gwendolyn found herself thinking about the Mecca building, where she had worked for the spiritual advisor, who was eventually found murdered in the building. She also had several other ideas for new projects, including a poetry writing instruction book, and a sequel to *Maud Martha*. Elizabeth Lawrence kindly rejected both of these ideas, reiterating her challenge to Gwendolyn to extend herself beyond the autobiographical. Gwendolyn began working on a novel, "The Life of Lincoln West," and she also submitted a proposal for Harper's juvenile department to write a children's novel, to be set in the Mecca building. Meanwhile, Gwendolyn continued to receive awards, publicity, and local support. Several recordings of her poems were included on the Glory Record Company's phonograph records, and she was often invited to dinners and ceremonies, and asked to judge various competitions.

On December 21, 1958, Gwendolyn mailed to Harper fifty-two pages of her novel about the Mecca, now presented to adults instead of children, with an outline of ten additional chapters, in addition to a group of poems. Neither Elizabeth Lawrence nor the Harper reading staff reacted positively to the novel, with Elizabeth pointing out the most obvious weaknesses, which included melodrama, unbelievable characters, and disorganization. However, Elizabeth felt very enthusiastic about the poems and asked to see more. Despite the harsh reaction to the novel, Gwendolyn felt Elizabeth's criticisms were accurate, and she was rejuvenated by Elizabeth's response to the poetry. Gwendolyn composed more poems, and on March 28, 1959, she sent Harper fourteen additional poems, several of which were published in *Harper's* and *Poetry*. Many of these poems differed in style from Gwendolyn's early work, as she had begun to experiment more with free verse. Although some of the Harper staff readers wanted to take out a few of the poems, including the one that is probably her most popular, "We Real Cool," Elizabeth was committed to the poems. She felt the book was an accomplishment, and that Brooks had captured the lives of "people beleaguered by confusions and terror, going about their daily trifling businesses, finding in the clichés of existence the nourishment necessary to endurance" (Kent 133). *The Bean Eaters* was released with 2500 copies in the spring of 1960; Harper gave Gwendolyn an advance of $100.

The decade of the 1950s was largely defined by the struggle for civil rights, and the poems in *The Bean Eaters* depict such social issues as the integration of the school system in Little Rock, Arkansas, in which President Eisenhower sent in federal troops to combat the governor's refusal to allow black children into a white school in 1957; the lynching of fourteen-year-old Emmett Till; and the misguided, though well-intended, efforts of white liberals to help African Americans. As these poems included more specificity regarding political events, several reviewers accused the book of being too polemical, or "too social" (Stravos 165). Brooks later recalled that *The Bean Eaters* "had a hard time getting reviewed," and commented that a reviewer for *Poetry* "was very upset by what he thought was a revolutionary tendency in my work" (Tate 43). Yet many critics viewed this book as being crucial to Brooks's development as a major poet. The critic Maria Mootry points out that Brooks, by refusing to employ sentimentality or personal reference, was able to offer a rhetoric of social critique while still using high-modernist techniques: "This strategy allowed Brooks to 'insinuate' her truths rather than to resort to the old-fashioned didacticism.... It equally allowed her to move beyond an entropic exclusive high-modernist 'art for art's sake' aesthetic" (178).

Although Brooks was flourishing in terms of her career, her success landing her invitations to banquets, dinners, and other social engagements, on a personal level she was facing one of the most difficult events in her life. Her father, ill with stomach and heart problems, had not responded to treatment. He had finally succumbed to the illness in November, not long before the publication of *The Bean Eaters*. Gwendolyn, shaken with grief, wrote a memorial poem for her father that became the dedication for her book. Harper editors then changed the proofs to include the elegy.

Her personal life was further shaken when her son decided to move out. Although Henry Jr. was eighteen, his parents wanted him to live at home. After escalating conflicts Henry Jr. finally left and took a room at the YMCA. In the same period, Henry Sr. expressed his frustration about his own writing; recently, his novel had been rejected by Harper, and although the publishers expressed interest in a few of his poems, he did not have enough for a collection. Gwendolyn also felt troubled by her career: all of her books were out of print; a biography she wanted to write about Phillis Wheatley had never developed; a recent group of poems she had sent to Harper had received a discouraging response; and she felt that she had little time or peace in which to write. And amongst all of these troubles, a severe lack of money, as usual, threatened to upset any sense of well-being for the family.

STRUGGLE FOR CIVIL RIGHTS

In the early 1960s, Gwendolyn received recognition in several forms, including a CBS dramatic reading of her poems, a program that drew close to a thousand letters of support, and in 1962, President John F. Kennedy invited Gwendolyn to read at a Library of Congress poetry festival. She was also in the public eye when one of her poems, "of De Witt Williams on his way to Lincoln Cemetery," stirred up controversy when a radio station refused to broadcast it. The poem had been set to music as "Elegy for a Plain Black Boy," by Oscar Brown Jr., and WNEW, a New York radio station which had broadcast Gwendolyn's reading of the poem in the 1940s, refused to air it because they felt the word "black" might be offensive. At the time, "Negro" was the more accepted and preferred terminology. Gwendolyn vigorously defended the poem and the word "black," which she had been using long before it became popular; however, the radio station refused to lift the ban.

That same year, the critic Harvey Curtis Webster wrote a praising article on her work that appeared in *The Nation*, in which Webster compared Brooks to such distinguished writers as Langston Hughes, Richard Wright, and James Baldwin. He also wrote, "[Brooks] has never denied her engagement in the contemporary situation or been over-obsessed by it.... Of course she writes of Emmett Till, of Little Rock, of Dorie Miller.... Like all good writers she acknowledges Now by vivifying it, accepts herself and the distinguishing background that is part of her distinction. But she refuses to let Negro-ness limit her humanity" (Webster 19).

Gwendolyn and Elizabeth were pleased with the article, and now thought the timing was right to release a book of selected poems. Gwendolyn, with Elizabeth's feedback and advice, rigorously culled poems for the book. After much going back and forth between author and editor, *Selected Poems* was finally ready for publication. Released in spring of 1963, the book met immediate success with the critics and public, with positive reviews appearing in the *New York Times*, *Poetry*, and the *Saturday Review*.

In the fall of 1963, she began teaching a poetry workshop at Columbia College in Chicago, her first real teaching job. At first, Gwendolyn felt shy and nervous with the class; however, soon she grew comfortable in her position and realized how much she enjoyed working with young people. Gwendolyn impressed the students with her attention to and advocacy for their work. She encouraged them to finish school and to read as much as possible. She taught that in order to be a writer, one must read and write, but also, "a writer needs to live richly with eyes open, and heart, too" (Angle 146).

The decade of the 1960s was filled with tragedy and yet hope for social transformation, and eventually Gwendolyn's poetry, friends, and her personality began to shift, as she became more aware of and entwined in politics and social movements. The year of the publication of Gwendolyn's *Selected Poems*, 1963, was particularly volatile. On June 12, 1963, the Mississippi Civil Rights leader Medgar Evers was shot and killed, and four months later, four little black girls were killed in the bombing of a church in Alabama. Then President Kennedy was assassinated on November 22, 1963. This was also the period of the Vietnam War, which would incite protests, controversy, and turbulence. Moments of hope also appeared during this difficult time, with the March on Washington occurring in 1963, an event which would help lead to the passing of the Civil Rights Act in 1964 and the Voting Rights Act of 1965.

Attitudes were beginning to change within the African-American community and the Civil Rights Movement, and by 1964, "the Freedom Movement was losing much of its polite, middle-class character, as impatient black masses forced even conservative leaders to take more extreme stands" (Kent 181). Black artists and intellectuals began to focus on black solidarity. For example, the novelist James Baldwin became a fiery spokesman, rebuking white Americans for social injustices and pointing out the problematic relations between white liberals and blacks. According to Kent, although Gwendolyn began to question many of her previously held beliefs, she did not yet make any drastic changes in her political alliances: "Despite the variety in Gwendolyn's experiences, there were, surprisingly, no indications in the early 1960s that her life would be fundamentally altered in the coming decade as her racial consciousness achieved a different focus and she broke with the white liberal critical consensus that had guided most of her career" (153).

During this time of political and social unrest, Gwendolyn devoted energy to the Mecca poems, experimenting more in free verse and long lines. The year 1964, notably for such significant national events, was also a year in which Brooks was showered with recognition, achievements, and honors. Her work was recorded on a program on the BBC, and she was also one of five poets of honor to be invited to read at Chicago's Poetry Day benefit. She was also invited to President Johnson's Scholars' Reception at the White House.

Despite all of her success, Gwendolyn also remained a very local figure in Chicago, with many friends and admirers. Once the literary agent Lois Bauer noticed Brooks at a social engagement, and recalled her modesty and warm presence: "[S]he stood in the same spot on which she stood when she arrived. The people came to her. As she spoke, with sometimes a secret smile in her eyes and sometimes a sadness, we were reminded of this bit from her poetry ..." (Kent 174). Gwendolyn's close friends, and those who had only met her briefly, were drawn to her compassion, humor, and kindness.

THE FISK CONFERENCE AND THE BLACK ARTS MOVEMENT

When Putnam publishers inquired about publishing Gwendolyn's autobiography, she approached Elizabeth for her opinion. Elizabeth assured her that Harper & Bros. would be interested in publishing her autobiography; she also wrote something more shocking: "Regretfully I shall not be with Harper when your next book is published" (Kent 176). Elizabeth Lawrence, who had been Gwendolyn's editor for twenty years, planned to retire. After she left the publishing house, Gwendolyn would be placed with another editor, Genevieve Young. Although Young did not have much experience with poetry, she looked forward to working with Gwendolyn, and in time, the two would develop a mutually respectful relationship. However, the news that her supportive editor and friend Elizabeth was leaving came as a blow to Gwendolyn: "When I read your letter I felt weak and old" (Kent 176).

Curiously, Gwendolyn and Elizabeth's professional relationship ended not long before Gwendolyn began to formulate a different opinion about white supporters. Although Gwendolyn expressed gratitude for Elizabeth Lawrence and the role she played in helping Gwendolyn's career, mentioning her in *Report from Part One* as "[n]otable among other whites who have befriended me and assisted me," Gwendolyn also felt that her support from the African-American community was far more meaningful (77).

This movement of African Americans breaking with the sympathies of white liberalism had been growing among black artists in the 1960s, most notably with writers James Baldwin and Imamu Amiri Baraka (formerly LeRoi Jones). During this period of transformation, there were many writers' conferences that centered around questions of black identity and the role of the black writers and artists, and in 1964, Gwendolyn attended the University of California's conference on "the Negro Writer." The audience was a mix of traditional integrationists and more radical writers. Ironically, Gwendolyn, quiet and fairly conservative, shared a platform with Baraka, who provoked discussion by claiming "the Negro writer has to make an intentional break from the mainstream" (Kent 179). The attendants of the conference responded warmly and kindly to Brooks, and when someone began attacking Baraka, Gwendolyn suddenly jumped to his defense. Although this early conference perhaps began to affect her views, her political transformation would not occur for three more years.

In addition to managing her family and writing career, Gwendolyn continued teaching for various universities, and took a position as a writer-in-residence at Aurora College, Illinois, in 1966. She also stayed active in helping and supporting local arts and youth programs, and rose as a prominent figure in Chicago, recognized with various awards and honors, including honorary degrees from Lake Forest College and Northwestern University. Gwendolyn, now fifty years old, was no longer a mother with two small children. Her daughter, Nora, was now a young teenager, and her son, Henry Jr., after spending time in the Marines, was married. Like her own mother had been with her, Gwendolyn was supportive of and devoted to her children.

Gwendolyn's list of friends continued to expand to include prominent black writers and critics. In February 1966 Gwendolyn met Dudley Randall, a poet, critic, and publisher of the independent Broadside Press, at a reading at Oakland University in Rochester, Michigan, which he had helped plan. After reading Randall's typically harsh reviews in *Black World* (then *Negro Digest*), Gwendolyn was afraid he would be "terrible"; fortunately, she found him modest, mild-mannered, and kind (Kent 191). Randall, an admirer of *A Street in Bronzeville*, felt delighted to meet Gwendolyn. He immediately felt touched by her warmth and gentle nature, and also admired her energy: "She's so strong—vigorous" (Melhem, *Heroism* 70). It was the start of a long-lasting friendly and professional relationship. Soon after their meeting, Gwendolyn gave Randall permission to publish her poem "We Real Cool" and later "Martin Luther King," which sold for fifty cents each. Randall had first started Broadside so that he could publish his own poem "Ballad of Birmingham." Gwendolyn was impressed by his idealism and commitment to black authors. "My strongest motivations," Randall expressed, "have been to get good black poets published, to produce beautiful books, help create and define the soul of black folk, and to know the joy of discovering new poets" (Melhem 191). Later, Brooks would turn to Broadside for all of her publishing needs.

Although meeting such authors as Dudley Randall contributed to Gwendolyn's growing awareness of black independence, it was not until 1967 that she felt she truly experienced a radical transformation, "a turning point" in her life. During the mid- to late sixties, anti–Vietnam War protests escalated, with draft card burnings widespread, and racial conflicts increased around the country. The black leader Malcolm X was assassinated on February 21, 1965 in Harlem. Malcolm X, the black Muslim minister, had mobilized many in his movement of black separatism, until his life-changing pilgrimage to Mecca in 1964, when he embraced integration. Riots in Watts, the black ghetto in Los Angeles from August 11–16, 1965, left thirty-five people dead, caused substantial property damage, and brought attention to the economic predicament of the residents. Many devastating riots also occurred in 1967. The assassination of Martin Luther King in 1968 unleashed more riots, as well as collective grief and concern about the future of integration.

It was in the year 1967, amid this period of tremendous turbulence in America, that Gwendolyn attended the Second Black Writers Conference at Fisk University in Nashville, Tennessee. Gwendolyn and her friend the poet Margaret Danner, who attended together, were unprepared for what they experienced. This was not a typical writing conference. Instead, it was a life-changing event, a passionate celebration of black literature and political autonomy. The presenters, including Amiri Baraka, Lerone Bennett, Larry Neal, and Ron Milner, were all active in the black revolution, and they stirred the audience members with their zeal and commitment to both literature and to social change. When it was Gwendolyn's turn to present, she felt worried about the room's reaction. She gave a short speech, but spent most of the time reading her poetry, which received warm applause.

Gwendolyn later explained that at that point in her life, she had read very little serious writing by African Americans, and she felt that perhaps if she had been better read as a young person, such as being more familiar with W.E.B. DuBois's *The Souls of Black Folk* when she was young, then maybe she would have been more prepared for this revolutionary movement, which had been building all around her for years. But what was happening at the conference was a new phenomenon for many African Americans, as it represented a break from earlier, and popular, notions about equality. Now, in the 1960s, across the country, many black artists and black college students were moving away from the idea of black and white unity, and were now embracing the ideas of black nationhood and black revolution, adhering to the early speeches of such activists as Malcolm X, and forming the Black Arts Movement.

The impact that this experience had on Gwendolyn Brooks was tremendous. For the rest of her life, Gwendolyn would commit herself

fiercely to supporting and promoting black autonomy. She considered
the conference to be her awakening. Before that, she said, "I had been
asleep" (Lewis 176).

The Wall of Respect

Gwendolyn returned from the conference to Chicago filled with a new
excitement and energy. Upon her return, Oscar Brown Jr. invited her to
a preview of a musical he produced with the Blackstone Rangers, a
Chicago street gang. At the performance, Gwendolyn "was electrified,"
and she offered her services to run a poetry workshops for the Rangers
(Tate 40). Brown connected her with Walter Bradford, a Wilson Junior
College student who worked with the Rangers. Thrilled that the
esteemed poet Gwendolyn Brooks was volunteering her services,
Bradford quickly helped organize a poetry workshop. During the first
few classes, which took place at the First Presbyterian Church,
Gwendolyn spent time explaining the form of the sonnet, spoke at
length about Shakespeare and Donne, and in general, bored the
Rangers. Bradford later recalled, "I think, after a while, she got a couple
of yawns out of some of them. So she changed the format" (Kent 204).
Gwendolyn loosened the class structure. Instead of lecturing on poetry,
she helped the Rangers with their manuscripts, and also became their
trusted counselor and friend. The gang members were not the only
participants in Gwendolyn's class; other interested Wilson students also
attended. Eventually, Gwendolyn relinquished the Ranger work to
Walter, explaining, "The Rangers drifted away after a while, but I didn't
want to lose contact with them. I asked Walter to start a Ranger
workshop on his own—and I financed it" (Tate 40). Brooks bought the
group books and magazines, and funded the workshop for a year.
     She continued to hold workshops for the junior college students
and youth organizers in her home: "The house would open up, and all
kinds of writers, dancers, painters, and just anybody young would come
along in" (Lewis 169). The workshops were composed of "young
revolutionary Black poets who would form the first ranks of the magic
circle that enjoyed intimacy with and loyalty to Gwendolyn Brooks"
(Jackson 283). Some of the participants became her close friends,
including Walter Bradford and Haki Madhubuti (formerly Don L. Lee),
who had already published a book of poetry called *Think Black*. Another

a regular member was Carolyn Rodgers, who would be nominated for a National Book Award in 1976 for a book of poems. Later, Gwendolyn would bring her students' work together in an anthology, *Jump Bad* (1971).

Although the major purpose of the meetings was to discuss poetry, often the participants turned to politics and social ideology. The majority of the young people in the group advocated the same revolutionary viewpoints that Gwendolyn had encountered at Fisk. At times, Gwendolyn felt at odds with the dominant viewpoint, as she still felt somewhat tied to her beliefs in integration and Christianity. Although she encouraged the young poets in their energy and beliefs, admiring their determination, she later admitted that when she had read *Think Black* "she had difficulty in seeing some of the work as poetry" (Kent 207). Gwendolyn adhered to the necessity of craft and technique, whereas many of the newer poets emphasized message over form. The young writers appreciated her knowledge of poetry, but sometimes they grew impatient with her somewhat conservative background, and several heated discussions led to walk-outs. For example, when Brooks questioned the value of profanity in poetry, Madhubuti shouted, stormed out, and did not speak to her for some time. To Gwendolyn, Madhubuti seemed aggressively radical and outspoken, but eventually, he would become like a son to her, as would Walter Bradford. Although Madhubuti often disagreed with some of Gwendolyn's early viewpoints, he appreciated what she taught him about poetry, and felt she always challenged him to examine his work more closely and critically: "Their relationship remains the stuff of literary legend, reciprocal and encouraging. He and Walter Bradford enjoyed some of the deep maternal feeling and care that Brooks gave to her children Henry and Nora," attests critic Angela Jackson (284). And in the opinion of D.H. Melhem, the "single most important influence on Madhubuti's career has been Gwendolyn Brooks, who gave him moral, artistic, and economic support" (*Heroism* 88). Madhubuti later praised Gwendolyn for teaching him how to revise and be disciplined, admitting to D.H. Melhem that Gwendolyn "played a very important art in shaping my work" (*Heroism* 120).

Although Brooks sometimes disagreed with the young poets' statements, for the most part, she felt the students were teaching her—introducing her to a world she had not known and challenging her ideas about art and literature. Gwendolyn said that the students "were the ones who changed my whole life" (Tate 41).

In her autobiography, Gwendolyn claims that until 1967, the year of the Fisk conference, she had "sturdy ideas about writing" but that the introduction to the Black Arts Movement challenged and capsized these beliefs (*Part One* 73). Her friend Val Gray Ward remembered the fifty-year-old Gwendolyn's newly discovered excitement: "She was high, she was spiritual, she was like a little girl jumping around" (Kent 210).

If the energy and political confidence of the young radicals intrigued Gwendolyn, Gwendolyn Brooks certainly appealed to them for her poetic expertise, her kindness, and her generosity. As well loved as Brooks was as a poet, she was also loved as a teacher. In a poem for Gwendolyn, collected in the book *To Gwen*, Madhubuti wrote about the tremendous effect she had over her students:

> they listened & questioned
> & went home feeling uncomfortable/unsound & so-
>   untogether
> they read/re-read/wrote & re-wrote
> & come back next time to tell the
> lady "negro poet"
> how beautiful she was/is & How she helped them

The harmonious, intimate relationship developing between the aspiring poets and Gwendolyn, and Gwendolyn's shifting and then solidifying attitudes about literature and politics, all seemed to be symbolized with the dedication of the Wall on August 27, 1967. The Wall of Respect was actually part of an old slum building at 43rd and Langley Streets, in the heart of the black neighborhood, and its dedication was to recognize the achievement of the Artists Workshop of the Organization of Black American Culture (OBAC). Ironically, two weeks before the celebration of the Wall, Gwendolyn had participated in another sort of celebration for the city. On request of Mayor Daley, she wrote the poem "The Chicago Picasso," a commemorative poem for the gigantic steel sculpture to be unveiled at the Civic Center. Over the span of her career, Gwendolyn wrote many commissioned poems for the city. When she attended the widely publicized and well-funded Picasso unveiling ceremony, along with mostly white social and business dignitaries, she read her poem of dedication before an audience of 50,000. Conversely, at the dedication for the mural the Wall of Respect, for which Gwendolyn had also composed a dedicating poem, no civic leaders showed up, and the event was completely ignored by the press. "'The Chicago Picasso' and 'The Wall' illustrate how completely Gwendolyn Brooks faced the dilemma of a divided Chicago," writes Williams. "Accepted and praised by the city's elite, she nonetheless gave voice to the inarticulate of her urban community and assured posterity to the would-be losers" (49).

The Wall of Respect was the wall of a slum building, which the city would later demolish, that had been painted with a mural of portraits of African Americans, honoring such people as W.E.B. DuBois, Malcolm X, Ornette Colemen, John Coltrane, LeRoi Jones, and Nina Simone, among many others, including Gwendolyn Brooks. On dedication day, Gwendolyn participated in the ceremonies, and after the day's event, the young writers took Gwendolyn to a bar across the street called the Playboy Lounge. One of the poets went to the front of the bar and told the patrons, "Say, folks, we're going to lay some poetry on you" (Stravos 152). This was Gwendolyn's first encounter of bringing poetry into the streets and beyond the literary community, and it left a lasting impression on her, inspiring her with new ideas about how to approach her work.

IN THE MECCA

Gwendolyn's experiences with the Rangers and the young poets, everyday domestic life, political events, and the setting of the South Side all fed into the development of the Mecca poems, which she had been thinking about and composing since 1954. The idea for the book was first conceived as a young-adult novel, then changed to an adult novel, and then changed to verse, which she had been steadily working on since 1961. With all of her work, Gwendolyn usually went through an extensive process of writing, rewriting, editing, and polishing until she was satisfied with the final version.

These poems reveal her increasing concern for social issues, while reflecting and documenting Chicago's South Side. "The new Black consciousness and its surging creativity; meeting Walter Bradford, the Blackstone Rangers, and the students she organized into a workshop—

these register in the style and matter of *In the Mecca*," suggests Melhem (154). The book concerns the building where Gwendolyn had once worked for the spiritual advisor, and portrays people who have been dispossessed and ignored by society. The actual Mecca building was constructed in 1891 as a luxurious apartment building for the wealthy. At the turn of the century, as the wealthy whites began to move north, the building became inhabited by the black elite. Then during the Depression, the building rapidly declined into a slum. "For those who trace the history of a city through the rise and fall of its buildings," Williams posits, "how poignant must have been the degeneration of the Mecca from the stunning showplace for the elite to an overcrowded tenement for thousands of dispossessed blacks" (60). The building, razed by the city in 1952, is portrayed by Brooks as a decaying, dangerous dwelling.

The book's title poem, an ambitious 807-line poem, Brooks's longest, traces a mother's search for her missing daughter, whom she later discovers has been murdered by a fellow resident. Other poems in the collection are dedicated to Medgar Evers, Malcolm X, and the Blackstone Rangers. When Gwendolyn sent the completed manuscript to Harper in September 1967, the staff was startled by the work. One reader called the book a complete failure.

Harper finally decided to publish the book, but wanted more poems to diversify the collection. Gwendolyn was unsure. With her permission, the staff sent the book to the retired Elizabeth Lawrence for her opinion. Elizabeth also thought the book needed more poems, and this time Brooks agreed.

Nominated for the National Book Award, *In the Mecca*, with its sprawling ambition, its prophetic tone, and its many characters, generally marks the shift in Brooks's poetic style, in which she abandoned the traditional forms of her earlier pieces in favor of free verse and also began to use more black vernacular. The poems in this book also show how Brooks is grappling more overtly with social and political issues. Gwendolyn affectionately called the book her "blackest book" up to that point (Kent 219). When *In The Mecca* was published, it sold an impressive 2,986 copies in the first week and received tremendous local support. The national reviews, however, were more varied. In the *New York Times*, M.L. Rosenthal cited that the title piece was "overwrought with effects—alliterations, internal rhymes, whimsical and arch observations," yet conceded the poem "has the power of its materials and holds the imagination fixed on the horrid predicament of real Americans whose everyday world haunts the nation's conscience intolerably" (27–28). In a mostly positive review in *Poetry*, the poet William Stafford stated that in Brooks's poems "there is this determination to see what is, not to opt for any falsity and not to abandon the risk of individual judgement either" (26).

Although some critics have characterized Gwendolyn's latter poems as being polemical, others point out that her subjects, from the early poems to the later ones, have not drastically changed. Brooks has always written about the lives of ordinary African Americans and the struggles against racism and poverty, the lives of oppressed women, and themes of racial pride. As the critic Angela Jackson attests, "Her style was not confined to literary fashion. She was not a confessional poet in the heyday of the confessionals. Nor was she a Black revolutionary poet, but an avid admirer of them" (Jackson 282). Many of Gwendolyn's supporters have pointed out that her poetry has always addressed difficult issues, complicated boundaries, and challenged social ideology, such as in her early poem "the mother," which concerns motherhood and abortion. Gwendolyn Brooks never escalated poetry above struggles of the people, and she had always participated in and supported the African -American community, as both a civil participant and dedicated poet, with poems about black leaders and political events appearing in her some of her early work. Although Gwendolyn gave powerful credence to the conference in 1967 for opening her eyes, in truth, she had always been aware of and invested in the politics of racial justice. "From the beginning of her work Brooks was well aware that racism was a powerful consideration in the American experience, and protest has served as a cornerstone of her poetic world.... She did not need anyone to remind her of conditions in the black ghetto nor to help her understand the depth of the effects of prejudice," attests Williams, arguing that there is not such a radical shift between the author who wrote *A Street in Bronzeville* and the one who wrote later books such as *Riot*. Brooks was always known for her sensitive portrayals of African Americans struggling to overcome poverty and harsh living conditions, and Gwendolyn herself acknowledged that although there were apparent differences, the themes in her later poems were similar to themes found in her early work: "I've been talking about blackness and black people all along" (Tate 46).

In various interviews after 1967, Gwendolyn stressed that her viewpoints toward America and the African-American community had changed, but disagreed that her commitment to politics had weakened her poetry—for example, the critic Arthur Davis felt that she had "gone 'black'" and "with the new blackness has come an increase in the obscurity of much of her verse" (Williams 65). Gwendolyn reacted against the criticism that in her post-1967 work, she allowed politics to rise above the craft of her poems: "No, I have not abandoned beauty, or lyricism, and I don't consider myself a polemical poet. I'm a black poet, and I write about what I see, what interests me, and I'm seeing new things. Many things that I'm seeing now I was blind to before, but I don't sit down at the table and say, "Lyricism is out." No, I just continue to write about what confronts me" (Stravos 151).

As her political convictions deepened, she became more dedicated to making her work accessible to African-American readers who were not generally poetry readers—which became a concern of hers after she participated in the reading at the Playboy Lounge. She spent much of the second half of her career trying to find a way to make the poems significant to the average or non-reader while still adhering to craft and artistic techniques. "I don't want to stop a concern with words doing good jobs, which has always been a concern of mine, but I want to write poems that will be meaningful," she explained (Stravos 152). Gwendolyn never believed that poetry should remain static, and she was constantly challenging herself with her work, wanting her poetry to change and evolve. While her early poems exemplified more traditional forms and language, her later poems experimented with free verse and urban black vernacular—and yet the changes had been building over time, and the new direction of her poetry was not the simple result of a sudden polarized switch.

APPRECIATION FOR THE YOUNG AND OLD

In 1968, after the publication of *In the Mecca*, Gwendolyn Brooks succeeded Carl Sandburg upon his death as Poet Laureate of Illinois. Gwendolyn would hold the position from 1968 until 2000. The critic Angela Jackson points out that in her thirty-two years as Poet Laureate, "initially an honorary title that came with no salary because her duties were expected to be minimal," Gwendolyn Brooks "created a role model of the poet laureate as vigorous advocate for the expressions of young people and as bearer of poetry to the people in all walks of life" (281). Among her accomplishments: she established and funded a yearly Young Poets Poet Laureate contest for elementary and high school in which "she honored students of all colors and backgrounds; she encouraged each of them with a special word" and presented prizes for $500 (Jackson 282). She also toured widely, participating in lectures and readings, conducting poetry workshops, and giving interviews. Tirelessly active in civil and cultural activities, Gwendolyn seemed to never turn down an invitation or request. She helped to publish young black poets, supported writing contests, and provided writers with financial help, even sending two young writers to Africa for $4,000. Now that her income was more steady, she was quite generous with whatever she earned.

However, as her busy schedule and community involvement increased, her marriage began to deteriorate. As Gwendolyn spent more time with youthful poets, Henry, a committed integrationist, felt she was being influenced by their politics; however, Gwendolyn claimed in a 1971 interview that politics was not the cause of their problems. Henry was also frustrated with his own writing career and his ambitions to publish. Gwendolyn admitted that Henry had always been tremendously supportive of her career as a writer, though she also recognized the possibility of his insecurity: "It's hard on the man's ego to be married to a woman who happens to get some attention before he does" (Lewis 180). Gwendolyn never publicly spoke at length about the troubles in her marriage. However, tension in the household increased, leading to Henry moving out in December 1969. "I'm not saying I'm down on marriage; it will just not fit in with my life," Gwendolyn said. "I like being alone more than a married woman can be. I love being in this house by myself. I want to be able to give my attention to writing, reading, and doing whatever else occurs to me rather than fixing three meals a day and humoring a man" (Lewis 180). The two would be separated from 1969 until 1973.

Gwendolyn gave much credit to the young poets for exposing her to social injustices and to the politics of black solidarity, and these students often looked to Gwendolyn as an example of how a conservative could change her views, seeing her as "the sister who had come home" (Kent 225). For example, Francis Ward, an associate editor of *Jet* and *Ebony*, wrote an essay addressed to Gwendolyn, saying,

"You're home now." Defending her against "those meaningless, cruel little critics," Ward urged Brooks to ignore the white literary establishment, once her biggest supporter, and the critics who now deemed her work too political. "Forget them!" cries Ward, "For they know neither Gwen Brooks, the black people she loves so much, nor the new forces which are shaping their lives—and America's destiny" (*To Gwen* 132). Most of this young audience viewed Gwendolyn's post-1967 poetry as her most promising work. For example, in the preface to *Report from Part One*, Madhubuti asserts, "When you view Gwendolyn Brooks's work in the pre-1967 period, you see a poet, a black poet in the actual (although still actively searching for her own definitions of blackness) on the roadway to becoming a conscious African poet" (14), but he claims that post-1967 Brooks is "a quiet force cutting through the real dirt with new and energetic words of uncompromising richness that are to many people unexpected, but welcomed by millions" (13). However, Larry Neal, a young radical critic and poet, wrote a letter in which he thanked Gwendolyn for her contribution to the literary community, and also implored her not to be easy on the young writers. Neal worried that Gwendolyn was too fragile and easily overrun by the young: "Please, don't let some of us so-called 'young' writers intimidate you. You have done your work and you are giving us a legacy.... I know that the word 'craft' is frowned upon by many of my generation. But craft, to me, is still important" (Kent 227).

Many of the writers and friends of Gwendolyn's generation expressed surprise at the credit she gave to the young poets for shaping her politics. In their eyes, Gwendolyn had always been at home in her blackness, and a vibrant part of the black community. The prominent intellectual Lerone Bennett, who was also the senior editor of *Ebony*, stated:

> Gwendolyn Brooks has always been committed and lyrical and relevant. Before it was fashionable, she was tone deep in blackness. In the fifties, she was writing poems about Emmett Till and Little Rock and the black boys and girls who came North looking for the promised Land and found concrete deserts. In fact, she has always written about the sounds and sights and flavors of the black community (*To Gwen* 2).

Even in 1950, in her essay on the role of the Negro writer, Gwendolyn had suggested that black poets must not lose sight of their blackness. She expanded on this idea later in an interview with George Stravos in 1969, using the example of trees. If a black poet were to write about trees, she suggested, there was the possibility that in his or her eyes, the tree might also symbolize lynching, and this would differ from a white poet's observation. "[The Black poet] has the American experience and he also has the black experience; so he's very rich," she concluded (166).

Despite differences in how they viewed her, both the older and younger generations recognized Gwendolyn's success as a poet, as well as her vigorous commitment to art and to the African-American community. To show their appreciation, the diverse group of admirers created a "Living Anthology," in which writers, artists, dancers, musicians gathered at the Afro-Arts Theater on Drexel on December 28, 1969. They performed and celebrated on stage for about three hours in honor of Gwendolyn. Immensely moved and honored, Gwendolyn called the event the "most stirring tribute of my life, the most significant" (*Part One* 197). The live anthology was later recreated as a book called *To Gwen with Love*, edited by Madhubuti (Don Lee), Francis Ward, and Patricia Brown. Comprised of poems and exaltations, the book is dedicated to Gwendolyn Brooks by the black artistic community. In the introduction, Lerone Bennett Jr. writes: "This tribute grew out of a feeling of awe which a number of black artists feel in the presence of Miss Brooks' testimony. It also grew out of a sense of communal responsibility, out of a sense that the black community must now assume responsibility for the support and recognition of public monuments like Gwendolyn Brooks" (*To Gwen* 2).

A DEEPENING OF POLITICS

Gwendolyn felt enthusiastic about writing her autobiography, believing it would sell well, although her new editor, Genevieve Young, cautioned her, as Elizabeth Lawrence once had, not to not get her hopes up. Still, in 1969, Brooks withdrew from teaching to fully devote herself to writing her autobiography. For the last six years, Gwendolyn had been teaching at various colleges, including Northeastern Illinois University, Elmhurst College, Columbia University in Chicago, Clay College of New York, and the University of Wisconsin. Now, to devote herself to writing her autobiography, she turned down many lucrative offers to teach from schools such as the University of Washington, the University of Wisconsin, and Northwestern University, among others. She also stood to lose an income of approximately $38,000 from local teaching opportunities, including full- and part-time.

In the fall of 1970, after the departure of her editor, Genevieve Young, Gwendolyn surprised Harper—now Harper & Row—by hiring an aggressive agent, Roslyn Targ, who approached the publishing house about Brooks's foreign publications, and also demanded that the publishing rights revert back to Brooks. To prevent such a reversion, Harper editors offered to publish all of Brooks's work in a single volume, an omnibus of her work, *The World of Gwendolyn Brooks*, which would be the last book of Gwendolyn's to be published by Harper. As tension between Harper editors and Targ increased, Brooks then startled the publishing house again when the staff found out, through a *New York Times* report, that she planned to switch publishers.

After publishing over thirty-five years of work with Harper & Row, Gwendolyn left her longtime publisher to go to Broadside Press, a small black press from Detroit, operated by her friend Dudley Randall. Broadside, which would now be her primary publisher, also agreed to publish her autobiography. In *Poetry and the Heroic Voice*, the critic D.H. Melhem stresses the importance of this move: "Brooks's gesture of commitment to Black solidarity meant leaving a secure position without any financial guarantees" (13). This obvious political move to the small black press surprised even her close friends, especially in this particular time period, when many African-American authors were seeking out larger presses.

Thus, Gwendolyn's allegiance to a black press and her current poetry reflected her devotion to black solidarity and to her ideology. *Riot* (1969), a poem in three parts that focuses on the riots in Chicago following the assassination of Martin Luther King in 1968, was the first to be published by Broadside Press. *Family Pictures* (1970) followed, which includes the poem "The Life of Lincoln West," which had once been the idea for an unfinished novel. Both books, heavily influenced by social and political events, and appearing during the peak of the progressive mood of the Civil Rights Movement, also reflect Gwendolyn's desire to reach the masses with more accessible poems.

Once feeling too shy to agree to interviews, Gwendolyn now felt driven to speak out about literature, politics, and black identity. For example, in a 1971 interview in *Essence*, she told Ida Lewis that she no longer believed in integration as an attainable goal. She said that in the 1940s and 1950s, when many of her friends were white, she had been naïvely hopeful for total equality among blacks and whites, and had believed that "[a]ll we had to do was keep in appealing to the whites to help us, and they would" (Lewis 175). Gwendolyn again named the Fisk Conference as the impetus for her "awakening." For the first time, she said, she realized "the thing to stress was black solidarity and pride in one's brothers and sisters" (Lewis 176). Gwendolyn made it obvious that she no longer sought the support of the white literary establishment: "Whites are not going to understand what is happening in black literature today" (Lewis 176). For the first twenty years of her career, the white literary community had been her main audience, and now some of these audience members felt that Gwendolyn was confining herself to black audiences. She remained unapologetic: "Today I am conscious of the fact that my people are black people; it is to them I appeal for understanding" (Lewis 177).

Gwendolyn's conviction that poetry must extend beyond the literary community to reach those people who did not normally read poetry continued to intensify and deepen. In a 1969 interview in *Contemporary Literature*, she stated, "[Black poets] are interested in speaking to black people, and especially do they want to reach those people who would never go into a bookstore and buy a $4.95 volume of poetry written by *any* one" (Stravos 149). Two years later Gwendolyn again spoke about the success of reading poetry in a bar: "My idea is that we have got to reach the audience the poets are reaching by going to taverns. I've been with them, and I've seen how that happens—how the drinking comes to a stop so that people can hear the words, words which are relevant to *them*" (Lewis 181). She asserted that she did not want to write "Ezra Pound poetry," that she did not want her poetry to be considered elitist (Stravos 153). While Gwendolyn once said that she did not intend to preach in her poetry, she also said she would not be opposed to her poems being able to teach her audience something (Stravos 160). Although some literary critics have argued that Gwendolyn Brooks sacrificed formal complexity for polemical messages in her later work, others have praised her "fundamental commitment to both the modernist aesthetics of art and the common ideal of social justice" (Mootry 1). Over the span of her career, Gwendolyn would read her work in schools, taverns, and prisons, always honing her style so that she could reach a black non-literary audience: "This is what I'm fighting for now in my work, for an *expression* relevant to all manner of blacks, poems I could take into a tavern, into the street, into the halls of a housing project. I don't want to say these poems have to be simple, but I want to *clarify* my language. I want these poems to be free" (Tate 45).

Gwendolyn's support for and activity within the African-American community, including her devotion to black publishers, artists, and children, was recognized with the opening of the Gwendolyn Brooks Cultural Center at Western Illinois University in 1970. A year later she started an annual magazine, *The Black Position*, the first issue featuring articles by Dudley Randall, Haki Madhubuti, Larry Neal, and Hoyt W. Fuller, and she also made her first pilgrimage to East Africa, a transforming experience that deepened her sense of her African heritage: "I tell myself, 'I don't care what *any*body says; this is BLACKland—and I am *black*'" (*Part One* 87).

During the same year, Gwendolyn returned to teaching. She was offered a one-year appointment as Distinguished Professor of the Arts at the City College of New York. Among her colleagues were the acclaimed novelists Joseph Heller and John Hawkes. The critic D.H. Melhem, who has published several articles and books about Gwendolyn, was then her student: "I recall her entering the classroom: alert, elegant, slim, her lustrous skin a deep brown, expressive eyes and hands like those in a painting by El Greco, a woman charged with enormous vitality" (*Heroism* 11). Gwendolyn's generosity, conviction, and sharp sense of humor were immediately apparent to those who met her. Whereas before, in the early years of her career, Gwendolyn had been shy in public, now "she seemed warm and self-assured" (11). When she gave a reading, Melhem recalls, "This was no ordinary reading. It was an urgent reaching out, especially to Black members of the audience" (11). Gwendolyn's stirring presence and her powerful voice, which could be soft, tremulous, or resounding, easily captured her audience.

Not wanting to leave Chicago, Gwendolyn took commuter flights each week to and from New York for her teaching job, but on Christmas Day, 1971, she suffered a mild coronary heart attack, similar to one that she had experienced five years before. To preserve her own health and strength, Gwendolyn knew she must give up this strenuous schedule. She withdrew from teaching and returned to her home in Chicago, resting and preparing her autobiography for publication.

In 1971 Gwendolyn was commissioned by *Ebony* magazine to report on black life in Montgomery, Alabama. She spent a week talking to strangers at bus stations and stopping them on street corners, and the result of her findings took shape in "verse journalism": a 677-line poem called "In Montgomery," that reveals the racism and also the apathy of the town (*Poetry and the Heroic Voice* 219). Following this work, her autobiography *Report from Part One*, published by Broadside Press, appeared in 1972. Documenting her childhood, her family, and her development as a poet, Gwendolyn also focuses on the transformation of her politics after her experience at the Fisk Conference. As *Report from Part One* advocates black solidarity, Gwendolyn urges her audience, "I want blacks—*right now*—to forge a black synthesis, a black union: so tight that each black may be relied on to protect, enjoy, listen to, and warmly curry his fellows" (91).

The mood of the 1970s, however, proved to be much different than the mood of the 1960s. It was the end of the Vietnam War, and also a period of government corruption, culminating with the Watergate scandal and the resignation of President Nixon in 1974. Much of the activism of the sixties transformed into a national skepticism and weariness, and these attitudes also affected the African-American community. Gwendolyn found the changes in attitudes serious and disturbing, and in her poetry she voiced her concerns and tried to reclaim the power of the Black Arts Movement.

The 1970s also brought changes to her personal life. After four years of separation, Gwendolyn and Henry reconciled in 1973. Gwendolyn decided to take the initiative to work out their troubles when she called Henry and invited him to her mother's 85th birthday. She knew that Keziah, a strong advocate of her daughter's marriage, would appreciate seeing her son-in-law at the celebration. Gwendolyn and Henry spoke on the phone about poetry and literature, the way they used to, and then began to see more of each other. Their marriage restored, Gwendolyn and Henry traveled together to London, Ghana, and France.

Although Gwendolyn may have eased her mother's worry about her marriage, she could not ease Keziah's grief when Gwendolyn's brother died in 1974. Raymond, who had served in WWII, died unexpectedly at the age of fifty-five. Gwendolyn dedicated *Beckonings* (1975), her next book of poetry, to her brother, and then she did not publish another book until 1980. Later, she did not feel satisfied with *Beckonings*, which she considered a transitional work, and thought that most of the poems failed in the new "heroic" style she wanted to use (*Poetry and the Heroic Voice* 232).

In 1978, Gwendolyn withdrew from the public to care for her mother, whose health was rapidly declining. For most of her life, Keziah Brooks remained quite active and tireless. At eighty-eight years old, Keziah had also entered the literary world, publishing *The Voice and Other Short Stories*, a series of autobiographical pieces and reflections, which her daughter had helped her edit. Keziah had insisted on paying for the book's publication, and then Gwendolyn gave her an autographing party at Chicago's South Side Community Art Center, where $700 worth of books were sold. Yet, the losses of her husband and then her son were grave blows, and as time passed, Keziah's health began to decline. Gwendolyn felt that the event that pushed her mother over the edge was when her house was robbed in 1977. Unfortunately, the neighborhood where Gwendolyn had grown up had deteriorated over the years, the bright homes now dilapidated and its streets dangerous. The burglary devastated her mother. "She never did get over it," explained Gwendolyn. "We spelled her decline from the moment of that invasion" (*Part Two* 23). As Keziah spiraled into dementia and frailty, Gwendolyn moved in with her, nursing and caring for her, but she was unable to stop progression of her mother's illness. Her mother lost interest in food, became easily confused, and grew unnaturally quiet, and then was hospitalized. On her release, she moved in with Gwendolyn, who continued to nurse her. Both of her parents were Gwendolyn's most important role models, and she loved them both with undivided devotion. When Keziah Brooks died on March 14, 1978, Gwendolyn grieved deeply for her mother.

MORE YEARS OF SUCCESS

Wearing glasses and her hair in a "natural," and smiling broadly in almost every photograph, Gwendolyn, now sixty-one years old, continued to receive recognition and honors, and followed a bustling, busy schedule. It seemed as if she was always on the move. She helped Chicago celebrate Carl Sandburg's 100th Birthday Memorial, received an honorary doctorate from the City College of New York, traveled to France and England, and resumed her extensive tour around the United States, giving readings and workshops.

On January 3, 1980, President Jimmy Carter invited Gwendolyn to read at the White House in the company of twenty other distinguished poets, including Robert Hayden, Lucille Clifton, and Stanley Kunitz, at "A Salute to Poetry and American Poets." Gwendolyn chose to read her poem "the mother," the controversial poem about abortion, which had been first published thirty-five years ago. She was subsequently appointed to the Presidential Commission on the National Agenda for the Eighties.

In a bold move that echoed her decision to leave Harper in 1970, Gwendolyn decided to start her own press in 1980. At this point, running into financial trouble, Broadside Press had suspended operations. Despite the difficulties she faced over the years in funding her own press, Gwendolyn was determined to assume total responsibility of her work, and she listed the many satisfactions she found in publishing: "control over design, print, paper, binding, timing, and not least, the capitalization of the word Black" (*Heroism* 32). Gwendolyn's decision to start her own publishing house exemplifies her ambitious drive, and her continuing advocacy for black independence. She felt frustrated by the ending of the Black Arts Movement and what she felt was a breakdown of black solidarity, and she believed one way to revitalize the movement was to actively promote black independent enterprises. She wanted more black presses to be generated. It was important to build the black artistic community, she felt, and to not rely on the support of the white establishment. Of the white literary critics, she said, "We should ignore them," and felt that instead African-American writers needed to focus on their own community: "[Black writers] must place an emphasis on ourselves and publish as best we can and not allow white writers to influence what we do" (Tate 45).

The first book published at Brooks Press was *Young Poet's Primer*, a book of instruction and advice for young poets. Her next two books, *Primer for Blacks* (Black Position Press, 1980) and the anthology *To Disembark* (Third World Press, 1981), revealed that Brooks was still writing about black solidarity, although by now the black power movement had lost its momentum. Critics often point to these books as her most radical and polemical: many of the poems urge African Americans to break free from the repression of white American society, sometimes advocating violence, and reflect Brooks's frustration with the disenchantment of the Civil Rights and Black Power Movements.

Although Gwendolyn now directed her work toward a black audience, she continued to be honored by the mainstream literary community with various awards. Shaw proposes that as "her esteem rose among blacks, it also took on a new legitimacy among the white literary establishment, including academics" (38). For example, Gwendolyn continued to be invited to speaking engagements at universities across the United States, and received a great number of honorary doctoral degrees. However, it is also important to note that much of her later work, published by independent black presses or appearing in small anthologies, was often ignored or overlooked by white critics.

In 1982, Gwendolyn traveled to the Soviet Union for a conference featuring prominent Soviet and American writers, including Susan Sontag, Studs Terkel, and Robert Bly. The only African-American speaker at the conference, she spoke about blackness in her lecture. In her second autobiography, *Report from Part Two*, Gwendolyn describes a scene of tension at the conference concerning the prominent intellectual Susan Sontag, who tried to answer someone's question about what it means to be black. Gwendolyn felt that Sontag, who is white, could not answer such a question, and according to Gwendolyn, Sontag then reacted to Gwendolyn with hostility.

Despite her extensive travels and her wide acclaim, Gwendolyn Brooks always remained associated with Chicago's South Side. It was the place she would always consider home. When she was a child, she had sometimes daydreamed about living in the country, but she'd realized later she belonged in an urban setting: "I feel now that it was better for me to have grown up in Chicago because in my writing I am proud to feature people and their concerns—their troubles and their joys. The city is the place to observe man *en masse* and in his infinite variety" (Angle 135). Unfortunately, her plans to turn her childhood home into a small arts center, as a tribute to her beloved parents and as a gift to Chicago's artistic community, were thwarted when the house at 4332 South Champlain was destroyed by a fire in 1984. Yet the destruction of the house could not erase her memories, nor her continuous dedication to the city where she had spent the majority of her life. Gwendolyn, like many African Americans, was thrilled with the momentous political changes sweeping the city. For the first time, Chicago had voted in an African-American mayor, Harold Washington. At his inauguration in 1983, Gwendolyn read a poem of dedication, "Mayor Harold Washington," and also read at his second inauguration four years later. When Harold Washington died in 1987, Gwendolyn wrote a poem in memoriam, which appeared in the *Chicago Tribune*.

From 1985 until 1986, Gwendolyn Brooks was named Consultant in Poetry to the Library of Congress (the U.S. Poet Laureate). In addition to her formal tasks of inviting and introducing established poets for readings, she also visited schools, colleges, prisons, and drug rehabilitation centers. She often invited local poets and students to read informally in her office, and then would take them out for lunch. Never being the type of poet who writes from an isolated ivory tower, Gwendolyn tirelessly committed herself to Chicago, the black community, and young people. Not only did she teach at the college level, Gwendolyn was quite dedicated to bringing arts to children: she believed writing workshops should be introduced to students in elementary school, to cultivate and stimulate their creativity early in life. Over the duration of her career, Gwendolyn personally established a tremendous number of prizes and awards for poetry, funded student trips to Africa, anthologized work, subsidized poets, and supported black publishers.

As rights to her publications gradually reverted to her from Harper, Brooks arranged to publish an anthology of her work, called *Blacks*, under her new imprint, the David Company, which she named after her late father. Not only was Gwendolyn immersed in local and national politics, but she also was sensitive to international troubles. The turmoil and tragedy of South Africa led to her book of poems *The Near-Johannesburg Boy and Other Poems* (1986), which she dedicated to the Gwendolyn Brooks Junior High School.

On June 7, 1987, the energetic and passionate Gwendolyn Brooks turned seventy years old. The celebration and festivities centered around the annual Poet Laureate Awards, the competition that Gwendolyn had initiated for young writers in an effort to promote poetry among young people. At that year's ceremony, Gwendolyn also honored seventy of her fellow adult Illinois poets, using over $7,000 of her own money to fund the awards. For a birthday gift, her "spiritual son," Haki Madhubuti, surprised her with the publication of *Say That River Turns*, a tribute anthology featuring poems, prose, and reminiscences about Gwendolyn by other writers and her family.

In her later interviews, Gwendolyn was not only outspoken about black solidarity, but also about the role of the black family. Reunited with her husband, Gwendolyn felt that it was important for black men and women to remain loyal to each other, and that black families could rise as the foundation of the community. At this point in his life, Henry had published his own book of poetry, *Windy Place* (1974), and Gwendolyn's two children were also following their own creative impulses. Her son, Henry Jr., worked as a software designer in California, and Nora became a playwright and founder/director of a theater company in Chicago.

Outspoken about her feelings on marriage, in a 1983 interview, Gwendolyn told Claudia Tate that while she understood the problems between black women and black men, she believed they must overcome hardships and stay together: "At no time must we allow whites, males or females, to convince us that we should split" (47). She did not regret her separation from Henry, nor did she regret getting married at such a young age. She felt that Henry had been supportive of her career, and that now they had worked out their differences.

Most critics have associated Brooks's work with the politics of race, and for years her work was virtually ignored by feminist critics, some of whom felt uncomfortable, especially during the 1970s, with Gwendolyn's support for the Black Power Movement and her seemingly untroubled stance with its male-dominant focus. Gwendolyn did not seem bothered by this perception. In the 1960s and 1970s, she, like many black women, felt that feminism was mainly a "white issue." She said in 1971, "I think Women's Lib is not for black women for the time being, because black men *need* their women beside them, supporting them in these very tempestuous days" (179). Yet, Gwendolyn also believed in equal rights for women, and believed that financial independence was one way of demonstrating equality: "And while money as such isn't all that important, earning and controlling it is symbolic of independence— for me, for all women" (179).

As Harry Shaw points out, many of Gwendolyn's poems have also concerned issues of women, with even her very early work revealing "sensitivity to the rights and condition of women" (23). Strong female characters have often been the subject of Gwendolyn's poetry and prose, and feminist critics in more recent years have praised Brooks for creating complicated female characters. Maria Mootry suggests that the support of Gwendolyn's own encouraging, if somewhat domineering, mother and her beloved aunts certainly had an impact in shaping her ideas of womanhood and feminism (13). "Moving beyond the stereotypical images of Mammies, Sapphires, Tragic Mulattos, and Street Women, Brooks, from the beginning of her career," writes Mootry, "had offered multidimensional images of black and white women mediated by complex narrative and descriptive strategies" (12). For example, her novel *Maud Martha* describes the life of a very dark-skinned woman, eschewing the stereotypical "tragic mulatto" character, which at the time was a popular figure in American literature. The critic Barbara Christian agrees that *Maud Martha* was one of the first pieces of literature in which a black woman was presented "as an ordinary human being in all the wonder of her complexity" (239). She points out that the novelist Paule Marshall, whose novel *Brown Girl, Brownstones* (1959) is regarded by many to be the beginning of the African-American women's literary explosion of the 1970s, considered *Maud Martha* to be the best depiction of an African-American woman up until the late sixties, and that the novel was a strong influence on her own work (239). Clearly, although Brooks did not form an allegiance to the women's movement, she had been writing about strong, complicated female characters for over thirty years, and in her later years, she acknowledge the centrality of such themes to her work.

In an interview with Melhem in 1990, Gwendolyn was concerned that many black writers were no longer directing their work toward a black audience; however, she still felt there was ample opportunity for black poets to act as leaders in the community. She was a shining example, still active in the community, and writing prolifically. In 1987 she participated in Third World Press's 20th Anniversary Conference, in which she received various awards. She also established her own Third World Press award of two $500 prizes, the award named after her friend and biographer, the late George Kent. For *Poetry's* 75th anniversary, Gwendolyn published the poem "Winnie" about Winnie Mandela, which would then appear as a book in 1988. She also published a book of poetry called *Gottschalk and the Grande Tarantelle* (1988) and wrote another book of children's poems, *Children Coming Home* (1991).

In 1990, Gwendolyn accepted a position as professor of English at Chicago State University. Her list of awards throughout her lifetime was tremendous, and in the last fifteen years of her life, grew even longer. Gwendolyn was the recipient of approximately ninety honorary doctorates from American colleges and universities. She also received the Frost Medal from the Poetry Society of America (1988), induction into the National Women's Hall of Fame (1988), and the National Book Foundation Award for Distinguished Contribution to American Letters (1994), with a prize of $10,000. She became the first African-American woman to be elected an honorary fellow of the Modern Language Association (1987) and the first American to receive the Society of Literature Award from the University of Thessaloniki, Athens, Greece (1990). In 1994, she received a milestone award when the National Endowment for the Humanities named her its Jefferson Lecturer, the government's highest honor for achievement in the humanities. She was also awarded the National Medal of the Arts by President Clinton in 1995 and the 65th Academy Fellowship from the Academy of American Poets in 2000.

In 1996, her second autobiography, *Report From Part Two*, was published by Third World Press. This slim book recalls Gwendolyn's childhood, with a long focus on her beloved mother, as well as her trips to Africa and Russia, and reiterates her views on blackness and the current political climate. She addresses her decision not to join many of the black revolutionaries in converting to the Muslim religion as being consistent with her outlook on all organized religion—that although she supported others in their beliefs, she did not feel comfortable in belonging to any particular religious sect. Gwendolyn explained instead she followed the model of her father: "I rarely go to church. My religion is kindness" (*Part Two* 19). Although adamant about black unity, Gwendolyn repudiated any form of prejudice or racism toward other nationalities, races, or religions, stating "I deplore blanket detestation of any group" (*Part Two* 138).

In the last years of her life, Gwendolyn retained a chair at Chicago State University, where a professorship was named in her honor and where the Gwendolyn Brooks Center for Black Literature and Creative Writing was established. After her husband died in 1994, Gwendolyn continued to reside in Chicago, the city to which she had given so much. She was a teacher, critic, and inspiration to many. To show their appreciation and to commemorate her influential poetry, on June 7, 1997, over eighty poets and writers gathered at the Harold Washington Library to hold a five-hour reading of Brooks's poetry.

Gwendolyn Brooks, prolific author of poems, essays, and book reviews, was as tireless in promoting and supporting others' creative endeavors as she was her own. With all of her readings, speaking engagements, awards, and community involvement, she was one of the country's most visible poets. As much as she committed herself to poetry, so she also dedicated herself to the struggle for black unity and freedom, and her poetry often grew from her beliefs and experiences. As she states in her autobiography with such astute clarity, "Blackness is what I know best" (*Part Two* 127).

Days after being diagnosed with cancer, Gwendolyn experienced a sudden stroke. Instead of going to the hospital, she chose to stay in her own home. With friends and family at her bedside, talking to her and sometimes reading to her, Gwendolyn Brooks died at the age of eighty-three on December 3, 2000.

NOTE

1. Brooks adamantly preferred the use of "Black," always capitalized, to that of "African-American" or "Negro." However, because of new conventions, this essay will use the terms *African-American* and *black* (uncapitalized).

WORKS CITED

Angle, Paul M. "Interview." 1967. *Report from Part One*. 131-146.

Brooks, Gwendolyn. *Report from Part One*. Detroit: Broadside Press, 1972.

———. *Report from Part Two*. Chicago: Third World Press, 1996.

———. Interview. New Letters on the Air. University of Missouri. Kansas City, MO. 1984

———. Interview. New Letters on the Air. University of Missouri. Kansas City, MO. 1988

Brown, Patricia, Don L. Lee, and Francis Ward, eds. *To Gwen with Love*. Chicago: Johnson Publishing Company, 1971.

Christian, Barbara. "Nuance and the Novella: A Study of Gwendolyn Brooks's Maud Martha." Mootry and Smith. 239-253

Hughes, Langston. "Name, Race, and Gift in Common." In *Modern Critical Views: Gwendolyn Brooks*. Harold Bloom, ed. Philadelphia: Chelsea House, 2000.

Jackson, Angela. "In Memoriam: Gwendolyn Brooks." Wright. 277-284.

Kent, George E. *A Life of Gwendolyn Brooks*. Lexington: University Press of Kentucky, 1990.

Lewis, Ida. "Interview." 1971. *Report from Part One*. 167-182.

Melhem, D.H. *Gwendolyn Brooks: Poetry and the Heroic Voice*. Lexington: University Press of Kentucky, 1987.

———. *Heroism in the New Black Poetry: Introductions and Interviews*. Lexington: University Press of Kentucky, 1990.

Mootry, Maria K. "'Down the Whirlwind of Good Rage': An Introduction to Gwendolyn Brooks." Mootry and Smith. 1-17.

———., and Gary Smith, eds. *A Life Distilled: Gwendolyn Brooks, Her Poetry and Fiction*. Urbana: University Press of Illinois, 1987.

———. "'Tell it Slant': Disguise and Discovery as Revisionist Poetic Discourse in *The Bean Eaters*. Mootry and Smith. 177-192.

Rosenthal, M.L. "In the Mecca." Wright. 27-28.

Shaw, Harry B. *Gwendolyn Brooks*. Boston: Twayne, 1980.

Stafford, William. "Books that Look Out, Books that Look In." Wright. 26

Stravos, George. "Interview." 1969. *Report from Part One*. 147-166.

Tate, Claudia, ed. *Black Women Writers at Work*. New York: Continuum, 1983.

Webster, Harvey Curtis. "Pity the Giants." Wright. 19+

Williams, Kenny. "The World of Satin-Legs, Mrs. Sallie, and the Blackstone Rangers: The Restricted Chicago of Gwendolyn Brooks." Mootry and Smith. 71-80

Wright, Stephen Caldwell, ed. *On Gwendolyn Brooks: Reliant Contemplation*. Ann Arbor: University of Michigan Press, 2001.

AIMEE LABRIE

Gwendolyn Brooks:
Poetic Justice

Addressing a crowd at the Jefferson Lecture in Washington, D.C., African-American poet Gwendolyn Brooks stated:

> ... Blackness is what I know best. I want to talk about it, with definitive illustration, in this time when hostility between races intensifies and swirls; in this time when numbers of Blacks detest themselves and announce that detestation with amazing and multiplying audacity; when hordes of Black men and women straighten their hair and bleach their complexions and narrow their noses and spell their eyes light gray or green or cerulean—thereby announcing: What nature afforded is poor, is sub-standard, is inferior to Caucasian glory.

Though declared in May of 1984, Brook's proclamation was not a new one, but an idea that was present in her work from the very beginning and helped to shape both her poetic aesthetics and the choices she made during her life as a Black woman, activist, and artist.

Brooks was born in Topeka, Kansas in 1917, but her family moved to Hyde Park in Chicago when she was only five weeks old. She spent the remainder of her life in the city and has always been considered a Chicago writer. Almost as soon as she could write, she constructed poems (her mother claimed that she was speaking in rhymes by age seven). Her parents supported Brooks's precocious abilities. Her father,

63

David Anderson Brooks, an educated man who aspired to go to medical school but, because of financial limitations, was employed as janitor all his life, made sure his daughter had a place to write by purchasing her a desk of her own. Her mother, Keziah Cornie Wilms, a former fifth-grade teacher, also backed Gwendolyn, never questioning the belief that her daughter would one day be the lady Paul Laurence Dunbar. In fact, one of Brooks's formative moments arose from her mother's influence. When Brooks was a young girl, Keziah arranged for her to meet two of the most prestigious and well-known African-American poets: James Weldon Johnson and Langston Hughes. Both Modernist poets encouraged the young writer. Johnson wrote her, saying, "My dear Miss Brooks: I have read the poems you sent me last. Of them I especially liked *Reunion* and *Myself. Reunion* is very good and *Myself* is good. You should, by all means, continue you[r] study and work. I shall always be glad to give you any assistance that I can" (*Report from Part One* 202). Both Johnson and Hughes recommended that she delve into the poetry of T.S. Eliot, E.E. Cummings, and Ezra Pound—a stylistic device she was later admonished for—critics believed her penchant for emulating the white literary canon ran counter to her interests in asserting the difficulties faced by a Black urban community. Her encounter with Langston Hughes formed a lasting personal and professional friendship. In 1988, Hughes dedicated his collection of short stories *Something in Common* to Brooks. In turn, she praised Hughes in a poem she wrote and in her autobiography, *Report from Part One*:

> Langston Hughes! The words and deeds of Langston Hughes were rooted in kindness, and in pride. His point of departure was always a clear pride in his race. Race pride may be craft, art, or a music that combines the best of jazz and hum. Langston frolicked and chanted to the measure of his own race-reverence (70).

Brooks's first poem, "Eventide," appeared in *American Childhood* when Brooks was thirteen. By the time she was sixteen, she had published 75 poems in *The Chicago Defender* over a two-year period.

One of the major turning points for Brooks came in July of 1941, when she met Inez Cunningham Stark. Stark ran a poetry workshop for black artists at Southside Community Art Center. She was an exacting teacher whose classes required students to push the boundaries of their writing. From that point forward, Brooks's career as a writer gathered momentum. Her first book of poetry, *A Street in Bronzeville*, was published by Harper and Brothers in 1945, followed in 1949 by the Pulitzer Prize winning *Annie Allen*. Next came the autobiographical novel *Maud Martha*, then another collection of poetry, *The Bean Eaters* (1960). Next came *In the Mecca*, then *Primer for Blacks, Beckonings,* and *Riot*. All in all, Brooks published twenty poetry chapbooks, a novel, and juvenile books and was an editor for several anthologies, as well as being widely anthologized herself.

Her first book, *A Street in Bronzeville* (1945), allowed the world to glimpse Brooks's ability to move skillfully among blues, sonnets, ballads, and other stylistic approaches that established her as a writer of great substance. The publications that followed would only serve to solidify this initial impression. *A Street in Bronzeville* first illustrated Brooks's range in tackling more traditional forms of poetry, such as the sonnet.

In the "The Gay Chaps in a Bar" portion in *A Street in Bronzeville*, which portrays the experience of Black men in World War II, Brooks uses the sonnet form to illustrate the difficulties Blacks had while fighting beside white soldiers whose prejudice went so deep that they prefer death over being "saved by the drop of a black man's blood" (*Blacks* 46).

The twelve sonnets in this group have been compared to those penned by Shakespeare, Milton, or Keats. The tight conventions of the sonnet would appear in other works of Brooks', such as *Annie Allen* (which received a Pulitzer Prize, the first ever awarded to an African-American poet). Here, the sonnet appears in poems such as "First Fight, then fiddle," "the children of the poor," and "the rites for Cousin Vit."

However, a few critics, rather than praise her for her use of the challenging sonnet form along with other more traditional styles (her work has been compared to that of John Donne, Walt Whitman, E.E. Cummings, and Emily Dickinson), faulted her for emulating white writers. Many protested that her approach was contradictory in that her convoluted language and difficult imagery seemed written for a primarily academic, white audience, rather than reaching out for a Black readership. She was also criticized for ambiguity in her early poetry.

The "Annaid" section of *Annie Allen*, for instance, a forty-three-stanza poem, was admonished for its "lofty" ambitions, which some say were unnecessarily obscure, leaving the reader to puzzle out the underlying meanings of the poems. Haki R. Madhubuti, in "Gwendolyn Brooks: Beyond the Word-maker—The Making of an African Poet," while recognizing the mastery of the poem, states that it "requires concentrated study.... This poem is probably earth-shaking to some, but leaves me completely dry" (*On Gwendolyn Brooks* 84). In a 1950 review of *Annie Allen*, critic Stanley Kunitz faults Brooks for being sentimental and naïve, as well as imitative of white writers. "Furthermore, I do not believe that Ms. Brooks should be encouraged to pursue her cultivation of early Millay inflection." He goes on to say that "the faults are not faults of incapacity or pretension: what they demonstrate at this stage is an uncertainty of taste and of direction" (11–12). Critic J. Saunders Redding, in a review that appeared soon after the publication of *Annie Allen*, was perhaps even harder in his censure. "The question is ... whether it is not the penchant for coterie stuff—the special allusions, the highly special feeling derived from an even more special experience—-that has brought poetry from the most highly regarded form of communication to the least regarded" (7).

In response to these comments about her style in *Annie Allen*, Brooks made it clear that she was "just very conscious of every word; I wanted every phrase to be beautiful, and yet to contribute sanely to the whole, whole effect" (*Report From Part One* 159). In addition, she defended the charge that she seemed to be writing to a mostly white audience.

> Blacks didn't seem to be buying our people's work in great quantity, not even Langston Hughes's books. It was whites who were reading and listening to us, salving their consciences—our accusations didn't hurt too much. But I was repeatedly called bitter. White people would come up after a reading and say, 'Why are you so bitter? Don't you think things are improving?'" (*Report From Part One* 176)

To be sure, Brooks's influences in the early part of her writing career were primarily the white poets. In an interview with editor George Stavros, Brooks was asked if she had a literary model in mind when she wrote, perhaps Eliot or Pound. Brooks responded

My gosh, no. I don't even admire Pound but I like, for instance, Eliot's "Prufrock" and *The Waste Land, Portrait of a Lady*, and some others of those earlier poems. But nothing of the sort ever entered my mind when I start writing a poem, I don't think about 'models' or about what anybody else in the world has done (*Report From Part Two* 156).

In another interview with *Essence*, she emphasized that much of her inspiration came from Black writers. "I read Langston Hughes' *Weary Blues*, for example, and got very excited about what he was doing. I realized that writing about the American aspects of Black life was important" (*On Gwendolyn Brooks* 80). Her poem "Langston Hughes" in *The Bean Eaters* illustrates her admiration of him:

Langston Hughes
  Is merry glory,
 Is salutary.
Yet grips his right of twisting free (*Blacks* 396).

Other critics realized that Brooks's style was not either simply "white" or "black." Critic D.H. Melhem writes that "'Black' content, however, like 'white' content, holds properties common to all human experience and is no more exclusive or homogenous, necessarily that black or white form" ("Gwendolyn Brooks: Poetry and the Heroic Voice" 21). Similarly, Norris B. Clark, in his essay "Gwendolyn Brooks and the Black Aesthetic" from *A Life Distilled*, declares that

[S]he depicts black realities without brutally frank language via her black voice, a voice that emanates a conscious humanistic concern for others. Similar to 'great masters,' Brooks poetry does not tell us that there is evil, corruption, oppression, futility, or racism; rather, she shows us the tragedy and its relationship to individuals in hopes that we may learn a moral insight from the juxtaposition of beauty and horror, death in life.... (86)

Brooks's style continued to illustrate her adroitness in exploring a myriad of forms. She used the ballad, for instance, in poems such as

"Sadie and Maude," "when Mrs. Martin's Booker T," "Of DeWitee Williams on his way to Lincoln Cemetery," "the ballad of chocolate mabbie," and "The ballad of Pearl May Lee," among others. Some of the ballads utilize straight-forward language to address contemporary issues, while others exhibit a traditional poetic sensibility, as in *Annie Allen*'s "the ballad of the light-eyed girl" or "The ballad of late Annie," where she writes: "Whom I raise my shades before/Must be gist and lacquer./With melted opals form my milk,/Pearl-less for my cracker" (*Black* 90).

Melhem lauds Brooks for her varied adaptations of style:

> Brooks employs both a recast ballad form and the blues proper, the former in third person, the latter in the woman's confessional song. Speech and music commingle. The ballad/blues confluence displays Brooks at her best "Tuned Ear," at ease with Southern black musical and linguistic elements. The blues itself is the musical genre developed out of Negro work songs, hollers, and spiritual. (*A Street in Bronzeville: Gwendolyn Brooks, Poetry and Heroic Voice* 37).

At times, she adopted "ordinary speech," or communicated to the reader as though having a conversation with the reader along with the dramatic monologue address. She would use improper grammar to illustrate voices of the street, as in "We Real Cool." In addition, she spoke in dialect in poems such as "The date" ("... if she don't hurry up and let me out of here./Keeps pilin' up stuff for me to do./I ain't going to finish that ironin'," *Blacks* 52) and "the hairdresser" ("Think they so fly a struttin'/With they wool a-blowin' round./Wait'll they see my upsweep./That'll jop 'em back on the ground" *Blacks* 53). Her implementation of dramatic monologues is evident in works like "Negro Hero, To suggest Dorie Miller," "When I Die," "Queen of the Blues," and "the mother." In "the mother," the dramatic monologue approach allowed her to present an intimate portrait of a woman who has chosen to have abortions. Here, Brooks applied the direct address, which allowed the poet to speak through the mother. As in other works, Brooks did not present the issue of abortion in binaries by either condemning the woman's choice or condoning it. Instead, she introduced the difficulties of the decision: "Abortions will not let you forget/ ... I have heard in the voices of the wind the voices of my/dim killed children."

> Though why should I whine,
> Whine that the crime was other than mine?—
> Since anyhow you are dead.
> Or rather, or instead,
> You were never made.
> But that too, I am afraid
> Is faulty: oh, what shall I say, how is truth to be
>   said?
> You were born, you had body, you died.
> It is just that you never giggled or played or cried.
>
> Believe me, I loved you all.
> Believe me, I knew you, though faintly, and I loved, I
>   loved you
> All. (*Blacks* 21–22).

The mother takes culpability for her actions, will not complain about the circumstances that caused her to make the choice, and will not allow herself to forget. Brooks, using the dramatic monologue form to speak with the voice of the mother, allowed a human dimension to emerge around an issue that was then not part of the public conversation. With the direct address, she is able to show that abortion is not a choice made out of laziness or as a product of thoughtless promiscuity. Instead, it is portrayed as a painful choice that will stick with the mother for the rest of her life.

Brooks remained modest about her poetic acrobatics:

> I really haven't written extensively in many forms. I've written a little blank verse, and I have written many more sonnets than I'm sure I'll be writing in the future, although I still think there are things colloquial and contemporary that can be done with the sonnet form. And, let's see, free verse of course I'll be continuing to experiment with, dotting a little rhyme here and there sometimes as I did in part of in

the Mecca. But I'm not form-conscious (*Report from Part One*
157).

In later years, her work began to appear in free and blank verse, and to
lose some of the ambiguity the poetry had been critiqued for in earlier
publications. A portion of *In the Mecca* illustrates this looseness of
structure:

> Doublemint as a protective device. Yvonne
> prepares for her lover.
> Gum is something he can certify.
> Gum is something he can understand.
> A tough girl gets it. A rough
>
> Ruthie or Sue. It is unembarrassable,
> and it will seem likely. It is very bad,
> but in its badness it is nearly grand,
> and is a crown that tops bald innocence
> and gentle fright.
> It is not necessary, says Yvonne,
> to have every day him whom
> to the end thereof you will love.
> Because it is tasty to remember
> he is alive, and laughs
> in somebody else's room,
> or is slicing a cold cucumber,
> or is buttoning his cuffs,
> or is signing with his pen
> and will plan
> to touch you again. (*Blacks* 411)

Overall, one continuous aspect of Brooks's style is her absolute attention
to detail. No word choice, title, punctuation usage, or image is
superfluous. Whether she wrote in sonnet form, ballad, blues, free verse,
in rhymed couplet, iambic pentameter, with irony, oxymoron, or
apostrophe, she remains an artist of supreme precision who strives to
make every aspect of her work count.

In examining Brooks's use of symbolism, there are many images that underscore the recurring themes in her work. For instance, she frequently refers to the color "white" has having an almost enchanted beauty, whereas "black" is less attractive. The contrast allows her to address the prevalent belief among both whites and Blacks that the lighter you are, the more beautiful; the darker, the less desirable and, in some cases, the more primitive or animalistic.

In "The Life of Lincoln West," from *Family Pictures*, Lincoln is born "the ugliest little boy with fat lips, big ears[,] ... the vague unvibrant brown of the skin," (482) and later set against his white kindergarten teacher who is "all-pretty, all tiny vanilla, with black eyes and fluffy sun hair" (*Blacks* 485). He grows up with the word "ugly" as part of his identity, as it is frequently referred to by others as deeply inferior, a marker of a lesser being. A white man seated next to him at the movie theatres whispers:

> "THERE! That's the kind I've been wanting
> to show you! One of the best examples of the specie. Not like
> those diluted Negroes you see so much of on
> the streets these days, but the
> real thing.
> Black, ugly, and odd. You
> Can see the savagery. The blunt
> Blankness. That is the real thing." (*Blacks* 487–8)

In "Bronzeville Woman in a Red Hat," a Black woman shows up for work as a maid with a bright red hat perched on her head. The color red suggest a sort of defiance, especially in a place that

> ... had never had one in the house before.
>   The strangeness of it all. Like unleashing
> A lion, really. Poised
> To pounce. A puma. A black
> Bear.
> There it stood in the door,
> Under a red hat that was rash, but refreshing—
> In a tasteless way, of course—across the dull dare,
> The semi-assault of that extraordinary blackness.
> (*Blacks* 367)

The white woman is soon horrified when she sees "Her creamy child kissed by the black maid! square on the/mouth!" She hurries to disengage her daughter "... out of the cannibal wilderness/Dirt, dark, into the sun and bloomful air...." When the child does not run away, her mother stands

> [h]eat at the hairline, beat between the bowels,
> Examining seeming coarse unnatural scene,
> She saw all things except herself serene:
> Child, big black woman, pretty kitchen towels (*Blacks* 369–70).

In "A Bronzeville Mother Loiters in Mississippi. Meanwhile, a Mississippi Mother Burns Bacon," colors underscore the horror of this fairy tale–toned poem. In it, the "milk-white maid, the 'maid mild—'" stands in her kitchen, thinking of the "Dark Villain," a "blackish child of fourteen with eyes still too young to be dirty." The boy has been lynched after being accused of raping her, an act she's not sure happened. The lynching death, which her lawyer husband, "The Fine Prince" participated in, has destroyed their marriage and left her with vivid recurring images: the red blood of the boy, his mother the "Northern, brown black," "the bleeding headlines" of the newspapers covering the violence.

> When her husband strikes their baby,

> She could think only of blood.
> Surely her baby's cheek
> Had disappeared, and in its place, surely,
> Hung a heaviness, a lengthening red, a red that had no end.
> She shook her head. It was not true, of course.
> It was not true at all. The
> Child's face was as always, the
> Color of the paste in her paste-jar (*Blacks* 337).

When he leans over to kiss her, she is sickened to see his mouth descending "so very, very, very red." Throughout the poem, colors serve as violent reminders of the crime, the guilt she feels in relating to the dead boy's mother (particularly when seeing her own, living child), and the resulting hatred that blooms in her chest of herself and her husband for being part of the injustice.

Another symbolic use of color can be seen in the more literal exploration of the gradations in shades of skin: from cocoa brown to dark black, colors that are set next to a constant white aesthetic, the two frequently juxtaposed as a way to illustrate the deeper problems of racial hierarchy of color, even within the black community.

As a little girl, Brooks too was unaware at first of how color played a role in the way she would be seen in the world. Instead, she was a dreamer, one who "loved clouds, I loved red streaks in the sky. I loved the gold worlds I saw in the sky. Gods and little girls, angels and heroes and future lovers labored there, in misty glory or sharp grandeur" (*Report From Part One* 55). However, Brooks, who was darker-skinned maybe, than some of her peers, soon began to realize that this difference set her apart, even from the other Black children she grew up with. "When I was a child, it did not occur to me, even once, that the black in which I was encased (I called it brown in those days) would be considered beautiful. Considered beautiful and called beautiful by great groups" (*Report From Part One* 37). In school, Brooks found herself among the "lesser Blacks"; skin too dark, parents too poor, hair too kinky. She was a quiet child, not a fighter or one who attracted the attention of boys. "As for the Men in the world of School—the little Bright ones looked through me if I happened to inconvenience their vision, and those of my own hue rechristened me Ol' Black Gal" (38).

In "the ballad of chocolate Mabbie," Brooks shows what that experience was like. Mabbie, a seven-year-old girl with skin "cut from a chocolate bar," is crushed when the white boy she likes emerges from school with "a lemon-hued lynx with sand-waves loving her brow" (*Blacks* 30). However, it is interesting to note Brooks's choice of the word "chocolate," which suggests an inherent richness and beauty, though the child might not yet recognize it as such.

Maud Martha, Brooks's autobiographical novel, deals with a woman's growing awareness of how her color affects her. Even from the beginning of her life, she is aware that her lighter skinned sister, Helen, will have an easier time of it—have more dates, more opportunities, simply because of her skin. As an adult, Maud Martha even imagines how her husband, Paul Phillips, must view her. She believes that she is not "what he can call pretty if he remains true to what his idea of pretty has always been. Pretty would be a little cream-colored thing with curly hair. Or at the very lowest pretty would be a little curly-haired thing the color of cocoa with a lot of milk in it. Whereas, I am the color of cocoa straight, if you can be even that 'kind' to me" (*Blacks* 195).

Later in the novel, when she sees Paul dancing with a red-haired woman at the Foxy Club, instead of being angry, Maud simply notes that

> ... it's my color that makes him mad. I try to shut my eyes to that, but it's no good. What I am inside, what is really me, he likes okay. But he keeps looking at my color, which is like a wall. He has to jump over it in order to meet and touch what I've got for him. He has to jump away up high in order to see it. He gets awful tired of all that jumping (*Blacks* 229–230).

Children, too, were often used as symbols in Brooks's poems, exemplary of the discrimination facing Blacks. But Brooks treats the children with her customary complexity; they are neither the cliché vision of hope, nor utter victims; they are at once the most vulnerable and the most resilient representations of their surroundings. Literature professor Richard Flynn illuminates the ways in which children symbolize the dual properties of despair and possibility in his essay "'The Kindergarten of New Consciousness': Gwendolyn Brooks and the Social Construction of Childhood." He writes,

> ... Brooks's work has used the image and voice of the child to negotiate a complex poetic strategy that explores "childhood" as a position from which to critique prevailing constructions of class and race. For Brooks, the subject of childhood represents a means through which she can interrogate and unmask dominant notions of domesticity and child rearing as part of her own radical social and political agenda (*African American Review* 484).

Near the end of *Maud Martha*, we see how mothers must fight to keep their children from prejudice as long as possible. Maud takes her daughter, Paulette, to see the white Santa Claus at a large department store. Though he is kind to the other children, his warmth shuts off when he sees Paulette. Her little girl has noticed this reaction and wants to know why Santa Claus doesn't like her. Maud struggles to keep her daughter innocent of what she knows she'll have to face: that she's up against a world where a white Santa Claus can't bring himself to smile or touch a Black girl. She wants to protect Paulette. "Keep her that land of blue! Keep her those fairies, with witches always killed at the end, and Santa every winter's lord, kind, sheer being who never perspires, who never does or says a foolish or ineffective thing, who never looks grotesque, who never has occasion to pull the chain and flush the toilet" (*Blacks* 318).

In the "children of the poor" section from *Annie Allen*, Brooks, using the sonnet form, offers a vision of how Black children, from the start, are poised for disappointment. It is the parents, then, who must fight to forestall the possible defeat looming in the future of their children. "What shall I give my children? Who are poor,/who are adjudged the leastwise of the land ...? (*Blacks* 116)

> And shall I prime my children, pray, to pray? ...
> I shall wait if you wish: revise the psalm
> If that should frighten you: sew up belief
> If that should tear: Turn, singularly calm
> At forehead and at fingers, rather wise,
> Holding the bandage ready for your eyes (*Blacks* 117).

The mother advises her child to "[f]irst fight. Then fiddle" (*Blacks* 118). But not all of the future is a hopeless kick against oppression: "Not that success, for him, is sure, infallible./But never has he been afraid to reach./His lesions are legion./But reaching is his rule" (120).

Brooks make use of the idea of the innocence that only children embody before they are aware of the racism. For a time, they remain joyfully oblivious, as does the child in *Annie Allen*:

> But prance nevertheless with gods and fairies
> Blithely about the pump and then beneath
> The elms and grapevines, then in darling endeavor
> By privy foyer, where the screenings stand
> And where the bugs buzz by in private cars
> Across old peach cans and old jelly jars (*Blacks* 83).

Unfortunately, she will eventually begin to understand the limits of her experience: "'How pinchy is my room! How can I breathe!/I am not anything and I have got/Not anything, or anything to die."

As is evidenced by many of the poems examined so far, one of Brooks's central concerns is the Black experience, particularly as it relates to the hardships of an urban community and how its members survive the poverty, disintegration, and limitations of Black life. It would be reductive to classify her writing as *only* an exploration of these themes. Part of what has earned her a reputation as a talented writer is her ability to pinpoint the universal struggles in life: the difficulties of marriage, love, loss, aging, and the search for meaning in an often senseless and sometimes cruel world. She does not pretend to serve up answers; instead, she gives readers detailed snapshots of individual lives, revealing their inherent beautiful and terrifying complexity. For Brooks, life is neither strictly dour nor strictly sunny but something that humanity as a whole can relate to. In her own words: "I want to write poems where people can say, 'Yeah, I've had that feeling myself'" (*The Life of Gwendolyn Brooks* 235).

In *The Bean Eaters* for example, Brooks looks at the universal difficulties of growing old, as well as how marriages can dry up and become nothing more than part of a rote existence. An aging couple eats a meal of beans in their rented apartment, where "dinner is a casual affair." The sparse dinner suggests a lack of affluence, as does the "plain chipware on a plain and creaking wood,/Tin flatware." Similarly in "the old-marrieds," we see two people sitting in "the crowding darkness" remembering that the "pretty-coated birds had piped so lightly all/the day" and the "morning stories clogged with sweets." Despite their realizations of what's good—that it's May, and midnight, and "a time for loving"—they have come to a point where they have nothing left to say to each other.

Her poems illuminate the difficulties in love relationships, particularly for women, who are often disappointed by the men who leave. In "when you have forgotten Sunday," a woman speaks to her absent lover:

When you have forgotten ...
... how we finally undressed and whipped out the
    light and flowed into bed,
And lay loose-limbed for a moment in the weekend

Bright bedclothes,
Then gently folded into each other—-
When you have, I say, forgotten all that,
Then you may tell,
Then I may believe
You have forgotten me well (*Blacks* 137).

The title of another poem sums up the same disenchantment with love: "For Clarice It is Terrible Because with this He Takes Away All the Popular Songs and the Moonlights and Still Night Hushes and the Movies with Star-eyed•Girls and Simpering Males." Her thematic interest in universal struggles, particularly with love, echo the advice she gave her children, Henry and Nora: "About love ... Little can help you. In this matter you are alone, except for your secret and everlasting unfinished acquaintanceship with your own essential needs" (*Report from Part One* 64).

However, it is undeniable that the recurring subjects of her poems are primarily concerned with urban Black struggles amidst systematic racism. Brooks contemplates the difficulties in the Black urban experience by honing in on the violence inherent in living in a place marked by oppression, poverty, racism, and the rage stemming from being trapped in hopeless circumstances such as these. She looks at how the members attempt to dig out of the ghetto, only to find themselves coming up again and again against the limitations put in place by an entrenched system of racism and social inequality.

One way the violence is illustrated is within the community itself, where senseless deaths and violence are a tragically routine occurrence. In "the murder" from *A Street in Bronzeville*, a boy kills his one-year-old brother, Percy, in a fire he set ... "with a grin/Burned him up for fun" (*Blacks* 38). But the brother doesn't understand what he's done or the finality of the death of his brother by his own doing. "Brucie has no playmates now./His mother mourns his lack./Brucie keeps on asking, 'When/Is Percy comin' back?'" (*Blacks* 138). Furthermore, violence explodes between men and women, as in "the battle," where "Moe Belle Jackson's husband/Whipped her good last night./Her landlady told my ma they had/a knock-down-drag-out fight" (*Blacks* 55).

Perhaps one of Brooks's most disturbing poems is the first piece of *In the Mecca*, a collection of poetry set in a slum building on the South

Side of Chicago. The title poem exemplifies Brooks's symbolic use of children to represent corruption, as well as the violence within the cement blocks and fenced-in confines of the Mecca ghetto. Mrs. Smith's little girl, Pepita, has been kidnapped, raped, and murdered by someone in the Mecca. She is found under a cot "in dust with roaches" (*Blacks* 433). In her unflinching and stylistically matter-of-fact portrayal of the event, Brooks writes,

> Aunt Dill arrives to help them. "Little gal got
> Raped and choked to death last week. Her gingham
> Was tied around her neck and it was red,
> But had been green before with pearls and dots
> Of rhinestones on the collar, and her tongue
> Was hanging out (a little to the side);
> Her eye was all a-pop, one was; was one
> All gone. Part of her little nose was gone
> (bit off, the Officer said). The Officer said
> that something not quite right been done that girl" (*Blacks* 421).

It is suggested that the murderer is not an outside interloper, but a familiar member known as Jamaican Edward. The violence lurks in the halls of the Mecca; halls crowded with crazy women, addicts, criminals, and prostitutes alongside children, mothers, families, janitor, butchers, secretaries. It is a place of still-born babies, fat gray rats, scurrying cockroaches, so overrun with chaos that not even the atrocious death of Pepita can phase the residents. More accurately, they cannot give in to fear. Their silence and acceptance are a matter of survival. "If/you scream, you're marked 'insane.' But silence is a *place* in which to scream! Hush" (*Blacks* 428).

John Lowney in his analysis of *In the Mecca*, "A Material Collapse that is Construction," notes that "the incipient violence that constantly threatens their existence is likewise no confined to an urban slum; it is instead endemic to a nation structure by racial oppression" (116).

But the violence is a microcosm of the larger outside forces. For example, "The Chicago *Defender* Sends a Man to Little Rock" describes the desegregation of schools in Little Rock, where grown men and women spit and throw refuse at the children attempting to walk into school. "... scythe/of men harassing brownish girls./(The bows and barrettes in the curls/And braids declined away from joy)" (*Blacks* 348). Likewise, "The Ballad of Rudolph Reed" narrates a tale of the harassment of a family at the hands of white men who throw rocks at their home. On the third night of the attacks, a shard of glass from a broken window pierces the face of Reed's little girl, Mable. Furious, Rudolph runs into the night to confront the men, a .34 in one hand and a butcher knife in the other, attacking four of the men before he is killed and subsequently kicked by his neighbor's kick who call him "Nigger." Back at the Reed home: "Small Mabel whimpered all night long/For calling herself the cause./Her oak-eyed mother did no thing/But change the bloody gauze" (*Blacks* 378).

From the violence and hopelessness of these situations arises the Black male anti-hero who desperately wishes for things that, because of his social standing, he has very little chance of obtaining. In "The Sundays of Satin-Legs Smith," Satin-Legs owns a wardrobe that serves as a stand-in for literal wealth—"... wonder-suits in yellow and in wine,/Sarcastic green and zebra-stripped cobalt./All drapes. With shoulder padding that is wide/And cocky and determined is his pride;/Ballooning pants that taper off to ends/Scheduled to choke precisely" (*Blacks* 43–44). Later, an explanation of where this penchant for "things" originates:

> The past of his ancestors lean against
> Him. Crowd him. Fog out his identity.
> Hundreds of hungers mingle with his own
> Hundreds of voices advise so dexterously
> He quite considers his reactions his
> Judges he walks most powerfully alone
> That everything is—simply what it is (*Blacks* 146).

"We Real Cool," (subtitled "The Pool Players. Seven at the Golden Shovel") echoes the oppression of the ghetto, centering on seven school dropouts who roam dark streets, "sing sin," drink, and ultimately die young. A frequently anthologized poem, "We Real Cool" is deceptively simple:

> We real cool. We
> Left school. We

Lurk late. We
Strike straight. We

Sing sin. We
Thin gin. We

Jazz June. We
Die soon (*Blacks* 331).

The "we" repeated is the disaffected Black youth of the neighborhood.
The speakers at first come across as tough; they have street smarts; they
are not oblivious to what awaits them outside. In some ways, the only
right or "cool" way to die is to go out fighting. We see the proud
posturing of the Black men, their jaded perspective. Ultimately, though,
their attitude is not meant to be seen as "cool," but to illustrate that
many young Black males do not survive into adulthood.

The men in Brooks's poems also have difficulty merging into this
"new" world and of leaving behind their own histories. Take, for
instance, additional lines from "The Sundays of Satin-Legs Smith:" "he
sees and does not see the broken windows/Hiding their shame with
newsprint; the little girl/With ribbon decking wornness, the little
boy/Wearing trousers with the decentness patch" (*Blacks* 45). The men
try on expensive suits, drive flashy cars, and date light-skinned women in
an attempt to acquire the security of wealth they may never obtain.

Ultimately, the violence within and without the community leads
to a rage that, if uncontained, could create even more desperate
circumstances. The title poem from *Riot* opens with a quote from Martin
Luther King, Jr.: "A riot is a language of the unheard." The riot and
ensuing carnage suggests that such an uprising can be followed by
greater destruction, not just in a literal sense but within the psyche of the
Black community. However, Brooks again does not suggest that it is a
question of whether to rise up or lie down and wait. Even as she
illustrates the futility of the riot, she acknowledges, that it does not arise
out of nowhere. From "The 3rd Sermon on the Warpland"

A clean riot is not one in which little rioters
Long-stomped, long straddled, BEANLESS
But knowing no Why

Go steal in hell
A radio, sit to hear James Brown
And Minus, Young-Holt, Coleman, John
On V.O.N.
And sun themselves in Sin.

However, what
Is going on
Is going on (*Black* 474).

In her later years, Brooks's themes would hone in more specifically on the need for African-American men and women to recognize their own beauty and value. Her political awakening occurred in 1967 when she attended the Second Fisk University Writers Conference in Nashville, Tennessee. Here, Brooks found herself both challenged and reinvigorated by what she encountered at the conference. The mood was charged with the growing wave of the Black Rebellion movement. About this time, Brooks writes:

> Until 1967, my own blackness did not confront me with a shrill spelling of itself. I knew that I was what most people were calling "a Negro" I called myself that, although always the word fell awkwardly on a poet's ear; I had never liked the sound of it.... Suddenly, there was New Black to meet. First, I was aware of a general energy, an electricity, in look, walk, a speech, *gesture* of the young blackness I saw all about me.... I didn't know what to make of what surrounded me, of what with hot sureness began almost immediately to invade me. *I* had never been, before, in the general presence of such insouciance, such live firmness, such confident vigor, such determination to mold or carve something DEFINITE (*Report from Part One* 83–85).

From that moment, Brooks' poems grew to have political underpinnings (something she was critiqued for; some critics complained that she sacrificed aesthetics to polemics). Her poetry became centered on Black pride and the continuing problems of racism. In "The Leaders" (447), she referred to great Black men like

Martin Luther King, Harry Belafonte, and Malcolm X. In "the wall," a poem written just months after she attended the Fisk conference, Brooks described a festival held on Forty-Third and Langley on the South Side of Chicago:

> I mount the rattling wood. Walter
> Says, "She is good." Says, "She
> Our Sister is." In front of me
> Hundreds of faces, red-brown, brown, black, ivory,
> Yield me hot trust, their yea and their Announcement
> That are ready to rile the high-flung ground ...
>
> An emphasis is paroled.
> The old decapitations are revised,
> The dispossessions beakless.
>
> And we sing (*Blacks* 445).

Her poems also addressed Black women, calling for them to put aside the white definition of beauty and to take pride in their own bodies. She praised Black women in "To Those of My Sisters who Kept Their Naturals"

> You have not bought Blondine.
> You have not hailed the hot-comb recently.
> You never worshipped Marilyn Monroe.
> You say: Farrah's hair is hers.
> You have not wanted to be white.
> Nor have you testified to adoration of that
>   State
> With the advertisement of imitation
> (*Never* successful because the hot-comb is
>   laughing too) (*Blacks* 460).

Throughout her lifetime, Brooks was the recipient of dozens of honors: several National Endowment for the Arts awards, over seventy honorary degrees from American universities, a Guggenheim Fellowship, and the National Book Award, and she was named the Poet Laureate of Illinois. This list is a much-abridged catalog of her recognized achievements. She also worked as a teacher, promoted writing workshops for urban youth, and was an active member of the NAACP. In these ways, among many others, she put into practice her beliefs as both an activist and a writer, and continued to emphasize the sense of pride needed within the African-American community:

> I had always felt that to be black was good. Sometimes, there would be an approximate whisper around me: *others* felt, it seemed, that to be black was good. The translation would have been something like "Hey—our folks have got stuff to be proud of!" Or something like "Hey—since we are so good why aren't we treated like other "Americans?" (*Report from Part One* 84)

Brooks died of cancer on December 3, 2000, at the age of 83. In an obituary from the *BBC News*, Professor Sterling Plumpp, from African-American Studies and English at the University of Illinois at Chicago, is quoted as saying, "At a time when black people were being clubbed into submission because of their race, it was her eloquence in her poetry that got many African-Americans to look at their community, and to see their minds as something of great worth."

Never once did Brooks relent from her desire to speak out about the social disparities. She acknowledged that, while conditions had improved since before the Civil Rights Movement, this did not mean that Black experience had moved from the previous problems. Time, in fact, had not repaired the racism and inequality prevalent in American society. She knew that violence, gangs, self-hatred, early death for the Black males, incarceration, and a sense of bleakness lingered.

> But I must "announce" that there is an auxiliary problem. I must announce that many Negroes ... no longer want any part of even *wonderful* whites. They have suffered so many crushes that now they are turning to themselves (find 'white' there too and feverishly scraping it out!) And they love blackness. They make a banner of blackness. What will be the end, as regards this intensifying compulsion? I am not able to tell you. When white and black meet today, *sometimes* there is a ready understanding that there has been an encounter between two human beings. But often there is

only, or chiefly, an awareness that Two Colors are in the room (*Report from Part One* 137–8).

However, Brooks was never a poet or individual who simply shrugged her shoulders or who proclaimed that Blacks should resent whites or that the two would never find a way to relate to one another.

Up until the end of her life, her poetry was realistic, but also optimistic. The following gospel-like poem, "Infirm," from *The Near-Johannesburg Boy and Other Poems* (1986), exemplifies her belief in the fallibility of humankind (Black and white) and illustrates that despite the fear and violence in the past, the human spirit is capable of healing:

Everybody here
Is infirm.
Everybody here is infirm.
Oh. Mend me. Lord.

Today I
Say to them
Say to them
Say to them, Lord:
Look! I am beautiful, beautiful with
My wing that is wounded
My eye that is bonded
Or my ear not funded
Or my walk all a-wobble.
I'm enough to be beautiful.

You are
Beautiful too.

BROOKE KENTON HORVATH

The Satisfactions of What's Difficult
in Gwendolyn Brooks's Poetry

Gwendolyn Brooks has been both praised and condemned for her often mandarin style. Thus David Littlejohn, writing in 1966, could acknowledge her craft—"she exercises, customarily," he wrote, "a greater degree of artistic control than any other American Negro writer"—but not, finally, the results of that craftsmanship. "In many of her early poems," Littlejohn felt,

> Mrs. Brooks appears only to pretend to talk of things and of people; her real love is words. The inlay work of words, the *precieux* sonics, the lapidary insets of jeweled images (like those of Gerard Manley Hopkins) can, in excess, squeeze out life and impact altogether, and all but give the lie to the passions professed in the verbs.[1]

For other critics, the real bone of contention has been the fact that, despite her efforts to forge a black aesthetic, Brooks has practiced a poetics indebted as much to T.S. Eliot as to Langston Hughes (though brought to bear on black subject matter). This white style/black content debate can be heard clearly in Houston A. Baker's *Singers of Daybreak*: "Mrs. Brooks," says Baker, "writes tense, complex, rhythmic verse that contains the metaphysical complexities of John Donne and the word

Horvath, Brooke Kenton, "The Satisfaction of What's Difficult in Gwendolyn Brook's Poetry." *American Literature* 62:4 (December 1990), 606-616. ©1990 by the Duke University Press. Reprinted by permission.

magic of Apollinaire, Pound, and Eliot." Yet this style is employed "to explicate the condition of the black American trapped behind a veil that separates him from the white world. What one seems to have is 'white' style and 'black' content—two warring ideals in one dark body."[2]

Both of these issues are complex. Behind the former—the emotional effectiveness of the poet's meticulous "inlay work of words"— lies in part the vexed question of modernism, which under the aegis of T. S. Eliot has been responsible, according to Christopher Clausen, for "the decline in the American poetic audience" and "the disappearance of poetry as a major cultural force."[3] Behind the latter—the problem of a "proper" aesthetic for a poet wrestling with an artistic double consciousness—stands the still-troubled assessment of, say, Phillis Wheatley and Paul Laurence Dunbar as well as more recent poets as diverse as Melvin Tolson and the Armageddon school of the Sixties.[4] In the pages that follow, I would like to add to this discussion of the appropriateness of Brooks's "tense, complex" early style as it relates to black concerns and, more centrally here, as it does or does not justify itself at its most elliptical *apart* from racial considerations. I intend to do this by examining in some detail one poem notable initially for its opacity: "'Do Not Be Afraid of No,'" which constitutes section nine of the "Notes from the Childhood and Girlhood" sequence in *Annie Allen*, Brooks's Pulitzer Prize-winning collection of 1949.[5]

A succinct example of Brooks's complexity at its most revealing/concealing, "'Do Not Be Afraid of No'" has received little close attention. Those critics who have commented upon the poem do so only briefly and with the intention of explaining its problematic place within the larger work of which it is a part. Thus, Charles Israel suggests that the poem reveals some of the "moral and ethical lessons of Annie's youth"; D.H. Melhem offers two paragraphs arguing that the poem constitutes "Annie's motto," her refusal "to emulate her mother's submission"; and Harry B. Shaw reads the poem as equating "the high life with death" and admonishing Annie not to choose prostitution as the only alternative to "the death of no life," a reading that finds parallels between "'Do Not Be Afraid of No'" and other poems such as "Gang Girls" and "Big Bessie Throws Her Son into the Street."[6] If none of these readings confronts fully the interpretive difficulties introduced by the poem's appearance as part of *Annie Allen*—for instance, determining who is offering Annie this advice (the answer will affect one's assessment of the wisdom of that advice and its impact upon Annie) or establishing the connection between the advice offered in the poem's opening lines and the remainder of the poem (for surely the response to this initial advice cannot be credited to even the most precocious young girl, as the poet's use of the third-person pronoun indicates)—this is not the greatest cause for disappointment.[7] Rather, what one feels most is the lack of any extended analysis of the poem that would account not only for its "meaning" but also for the poet's stylistic choices and for the relation of both message and style to Brooks's concerns as a black female poet. I suggest that such a close reading reveals a style not merely justified by the poem's content but essential if readers are to *experience* (rather than simply be told) the truth the poem embodies.

"'Do Not Be Afraid of No'" begins straightforwardly enough by reiterating the advice of its title in two lines enclosed by quotation marks and concluded by a colon, which suggests that what follows will be a gloss upon this advice, the development of an argument in support of this thesis.

"Do not be afraid of no,
Who has so far so very far to go":

"Do not be afraid [to say] no" seems simple advice; indeed, now that "just say no" has become the lamest sort of response to social problems, Brooks's opening lines may seem not so much simple as simple-minded (they will prove to be neither). But certain problems arise even here: Who is speaking and to whom? Are these lines something the poet has been told or read (hence the quotation marks)? One can of course fall back upon the response that these lines are spoken by someone to Annie (although I don't find this wholly clarifying for reasons such as those sketched above), but here I am suggesting that for "Annie" one might—for the duration of the poem—substitute any young (black) girl" or, more generally, "anyone"—and here it is useful to recall George Kent's observation that in *Annie Allen* one advantage of the poetic form is to "move experiences immediately into symbols broader than the person serving as subject."[8] But further, to whom or what does the "who" of line two refer: to "no," its grammatical antecedent (in which case, why "who" instead of "which"?), or to the addressee—Annie aside, the choices would seem to be the poem's readers, self-reflexively the poet, or some unknown third party—who has "so far so very far to go"? And "to go" where? In life? One can be no more precise than that for now. These questions, however, are only mildly vexing because one presumes they will be answered (they won't be) in language similarly direct (it won't be but will tend toward greater confusion before somewhat clarifying itself).

Stanza two acknowledges that saying "no" is never easy:

New caution to occur
To one whose inner scream set her to cede, for
        softer lapping and smooth fur!

As noted above, the opening lines appear in quotation marks possibly to suggest they contain received wisdom the perspicacity of which the poet intends to ponder. For one thing, she knows that saying "yes" means reaching agreement, solving a problem, accepting a plan, a truth, a life mate: "yes" is at least superficially positive, resolves that often unsettling uncertainty and probable antagonism "no" involves; "no" leaves one in suspense, in suspension, dissatisfied, perhaps closed off from comforts and companions. To say "no" to something is not, after all, necessarily to say "yes" to something else.

But through stanza two (and beyond), what exactly is at issue remains terribly amorphous. The reader, aware of who has written the poem and the historical circumstances surrounding its composition, might conclude that Brooks has something racial to denounce but is couching that denunciation in self-protectively cryptic language. But what? Is the poem an example of what Gary Smith has labelled Brooks's "remarkably consistent" identification of "white racism and its pervasive socio-economic effects" on the black community?[9] If so, how so? Or perhaps the poem is not primarily racial but speaks of some political, economic, or ideological crisis on the international scene? Or perhaps this is a prototypical instance of confessional poetry that speaks of larger concerns only as they impinge upon the private psyche? If Clara Claiborne Park is correct in reading *Annie Allen* as "a varied and inventive sequence of poems evoking a poor black woman's progress from exquisite illusion to the recognition of a harder yet more satisfying reality," and if one recalls Brooks's early poetic successes (encouraged by a mother who "intended her to be 'the *lady* Paul Laurence Dunbar'") within the white world of poetry and subsequent break in the late Sixties with that world in favor of poetry intent on speaking to African Americans of their concerns and in their language, then the poem might well be read as offering an elliptical rejection of poetic success in white literary terms (as either the black T. S. Eliot or the "lady" Paul Laurence Dunbar).[10] Such a reading is possible, but without seeking extratextual aid one cannot say "yes" to any of these possibilities—and so the poem is already teaching the reader the wisdom of the provisional "no."

At any rate, the advice of stanza one is a "new caution" to one predisposed to saying "yes," a new word of warning whose wisdom has occurred to the poet. The "she" of line four may refer to Everywoman, but the advice is pertinent to anyone—that is, to all of us—whose heart cries out to accede, to surrender by conceding and so avoid unpleasantness and secure comfort, that "softer lapping and smooth fur!" This last phrase is a wonderfully odd and unexpected evocation of pseudo-desiderata that, in conjunction with "set her to cede" (which recalls the cliché "gone to seed"), suggests that "yes" buys the reader something that leaves her less than human. And here one recalls John Updike's remark that "a person who has what he wants"—or thinks he has—"ceases to be a person," is "just an animal with clothes on," as Brooks's images of lapping and fur imply.[11] But perhaps at this point the poem now seems more Feminist than racial, the combination of the feminine pronoun and the sensual, vaguely sexual imagery suggesting that women ought not sell out by acquiescing to marriage or a subordinate position in a relationship—although this is, obviously, as conjectural as those racial/political/autobiographical concerns hypothesized earlier. Whatever surrender is to be avoided, the exclamation point registers the poet's shock that such capitulation could even be considered for the tawdry prizes it would win one.

Stanzas three and four analyze and thereby judge the kind of person who could so easily acquiesce as well as the shortsightedness of such a maneuver:

> Whose esoteric need
> Was merely to avoid the nettle, to not-bleed.
>
> Stupid, like a street
> That beats into a dead end and dies there, with nothing left
>   to reprimand or meet.

Such an individual's need is "esoteric," not in the sense of being understandable only to a few (the poet has implicitly—through her avoidance of greater specificity—acknowledged the universality of the desire to avoid pain and to seek pleasure) but in the sense of being "difficult to understand," of being "not publicly disclosed."[12] To seek merely to "not-bleed," to sell one's birthright for a mess of ease, *is* finally difficult to fathom and rarely the reason offered publicly to explain one's ceding. For instance, to return (for illustrative purposes only) to the possibility of the poem offering us a feminist commentary upon marriage: a bride's "I do" does not normally confess to a desire "merely to avoid the nettle" but rather professes acceptance of a noble calling, honorable commitments.

However, as the reader moves into stanza four, "yes" becomes more than demeaning; it is also "stupid": a dead end where one dies. The "no" that typically may seem pure denial now becomes by contrast the means of opening one to possibility, of keeping one in motion and alive in a world where, yes, there still exists the chance of severe censure but also of further experiences to encounter, to undergo (for the experience "no" makes possible never loses here its sense of trial). And beyond the multiple apposite senses of "meet," one may also recall that "reprimand" derives from *reprimere*, "to repress": in death those fears "yes" repressed will indeed be at an end. In the context of the poem, "yes" becomes a denial of life, "no" implicitly its affirmation. Brooks is here advocating an invigorating sort of denial not unlike that "No! in thunder" Melville spoke of and which Leslie Fiedler has argued underlies all first-rate literature.[13] For now, the redefinition of "yes" and "no" these lines are effecting is perhaps best suggested by reference to Melville's famous letter to Hawthorne in which he observes that "All men who say *yes*, lie; and all men who say *no*,—why, they are in the happy condition of judicious, unincumbered travellers in Europe; they cross the frontiers into Eternity with nothing but a carpetbag—that is to say Ego. Whereas those *yes*-gentry, they travel with heaps of baggage, and damn them! they will never get through the Custom House."[14] But again, if the reader is unwilling to assent to these remarks, she is learning Brooks's lesson.

Stanzas five and six elaborate and complicate the yea-sayer's increasingly dismal situation through images and syntax themselves increasingly elaborate and complex.

And like a candle fixed
Against dismay and countershine of mixed

Wild moon and sun. And like
A flying furniture, or bird with lattice wing; or gaunt thing,
a-stammer down nightmare neon peopled with
condor, hawk, and shrike.

These lines are difficult to negotiate in part because the key to understanding Brooks's symbolic candle is buried—like the implications of "yes," whose consequences now seem a nightmare deferred—midway through a grammatical fragment (the poem's third so far, each hinting at the level of sentence structure at the incompleteness of the yes-man or yes-woman, at his or her inability to entertain a complete thought on what consent signifies). The key is "wild" and is underscored by the "flying furniture" of line twelve: in the face of present reality, "yes" is no more than a candle in the wild winds of dismay that will send one's (domestic) ease flying like tables and chairs in a tornado.

Stanza six's imagery is apocalyptic ("countershine of mixed // Wild moon and sun"), Bosch-like ("A flying furniture, or bird with lattice wing," this last a hopeless image of impossible flight), and violent with the predatory horror of nightmarish phantasm. At this point in the poem, the reader has been sucked deep into the maelstrom of the once-benign "yes." The language has reached fever pitch with its invocation of a neon-lit landscape "peopled" by condor, hawk, and shrike (also known, tellingly, as the butcherbird) across which "stammers" a "gaunt *thing*"—perhaps the yes-victim, perhaps her assassin.

So that the point will not be lost, the poet recapitulates bluntly in stanza seven. Earlier, such a direct, unambiguous assertion could have passed as so much lame rhetoric, but now it strides forth as stark summation:

To say yes is to die
A lot or a little. The dead wear capably their wry

Enameled emblems. They smell.
But that and that they do not altogether yell is all that we
        know well.

The reader has heard before—in the final line of stanza two—the exasperated sarcasm that reappears with "a little." This modifier is neither a crumb thrown to one's desire for mitigation nor a means of toning down the poem's rhetorical frenzy. Rather, it implies that yes-people have but a small transition to make from nominal living to quiet, smelly death, a condition they wear "capably," their headstones no doubt bearing affirmative "enameled" (protective possibly, but probably merely decorative) "emblems."

The case against "yes" complete, the poem moves explicitly into its advocacy of "no":

> It is brave to be involved,
> To be not fearful to he unresolved.
>
> Her new wish was to smile
> When answers took no airships, walked a while.

Nay-saying, as observed before, is not to be perceived as resolution, as a negative means (otherwise similar to "yes") of closing the books. It is instead a way of bravely remaining "involved" while vitally "unresolved." "No" engenders life and keeps that life in conceivably uncomfortable but nonetheless healthy motion. Although the specific concerns being addressed remain undefined even at poem's end, its final lines suggest that those answers to which allegiance may one day be pledged *will* come, but they must be worked for and may be some time in arriving (they walk; they do not fly). This hope, this promise of resolution has, one notices, been present throughout the poem. In line two, for instance, the reader realizes that "so very far" was actually not a feeble attempt to intensify the initial "so far"; rather, "so far" was qualifying "so very far" in the sense of "at the moment." Thus the sense of line two is not primarily that "no" has "very very far to go" but that, although it does have a long way to go, every day, every line, will find "no" closer to its goal. And after all, the poem is written in rhyming couplets manifesting consonance (a correspondence of sound implying agreement, harmony, accord), although line lengths and rhythm vary wildly, postponing for varying lengths of time that consonance (a consonance most readily apparent in those most regular couplets devoted to the virtues of "no"). Here, then, at the level of sound, rhythm, and structure, the poem bodies forth its message that agreement will come (though necessarily delayed) but must not be sought prematurely or expected as a matter of (strict metrical) course.

The poem's final images are clear and positive, sparkling with hope, cheer, courage, and newness (just as they introduce a new tone into the poem). They also highlight what should be obvious by now: "no" is safer than "yes," just as walking is (whatever airlines may say) safer than flying (with the walking nay-sayer contrasted with the dead yea-sayer and dead-end streets where motion comes to an end, while the airships, associated with the yea-sayer's wish for trouble-free rapid transit, recall the flying furniture of the poem's horrific sixth stanza).

The complexity of "'Do Not Be Afraid of No'" is, then, aesthetically justified because the poem teaches at every level of itself the need to remain actively engaged (as one must be involved with it) yet wary of reaching closure (as one must be when confronted by a poem that refuses too quickly to relinquish its meaning). No image easily elicits the reader's consent, which must anyway await one's understanding of each part in relation to the whole, just as one must assess any extratextual consent in relation to its effect on one's life as a whole. Similarly, the poem's terribly precise vagueness is likewise justified insofar as it leaves the poem open to speak to anyone confronted by any situation where a preemptive assent seems the path of least resistance (a message as intensely relevant for blacks in 1949 as it ever was before or after this date). Just as does Brooks's famous sonnet "First fight. Then fiddle," "'Do Not Be Afraid of No'" places stylistic resistance at the center of her message concerning the need for resistance at the social/political level. And if "'Do Not Be Afraid of No'" is still worlds away from the directness of, say, "We Real Cool," Brooks might be seen in this early poem to be considering already that stylistic maneuver Park discovers in the much later "In the Mecca" (1968), wherein the critic finds Brooks "los[ing] faith in the kind of music she had loved and was so well qualified to sing" but which "blacks now found unusable."[15]

At the poem's end, as I have noted, whatever it was—social issue, personal concern, aesthetic challenge—that planted the seed of the poem in Brooks's mind ("set her to cede") remains as indefinite as it was when we began. We can ask, Does she wish to urge "no" upon blacks too willing to accept token adjustments of the status quo? Or does she desire to tell women not to surrender their dreams too easily? Or to tell readers not to dismiss her work too quickly? Does she wish to say "no" to a poetic style already proving itself unsatisfactory? All would be provocative messages—and Brooks allows us to entertain each of them—but I see no special textual support for any of them.

"'Do Not Be Afraid of No'" works hard at keeping the reader involved with it by making her feel she has not yet fully gotten into it, leaving open a multiplicity of interpretive possibilities by neither sanctioning nor precluding any of them. And if this assessment is accurate, the poem reveals as well the wisdom of Brooks's strategy as the vehicle for black (social/political) content, for she knows, as do we all, that America will, alas, always provide situations demanding rejection but tempting us to acquiesce either because we grow exhausted and resigned or because the carrot on the stick is lusciously attractive. And beyond the circumference of these concerns, and to return to Melville by way of Fiedler, Brooks knows the aesthetic correctness of the "no! in thunder," a denial not circumscribed completely by events of the moment any more than "'Do Not Be Afraid of No'" is delimited by its appearance originally as part of *Annie Allen*. As the engaged, topical poetry of the early Nikki Giovanni or of Don L. Lee (Haki Madhubuti) suggests, the easy "no"—to racism, poverty, whatever—can make finally for limited art."[16] Alternatively, "'Do Not Be Afraid of No'"—which might now be seen working metapoetically—offers instead a timeless "no," a "no" applicable in any circumstance that tempts anyone with the desire to acquiesce. Thus, Brooks offers a poem that is both timely and timeless, which is, after all, one definition of a classic.

Indeed, logically, no ready consent to the poem's message is possible even after lengthy explication, for to say "yes" to "'Do Not Be Afraid of No'" is to imply one has possibly misread it. On the other hand, to say "no" to the poem is, willy-nilly, to act upon the poem's advice, hence to concur with the wisdom of that advice, suggesting once again that the lesson has been lost upon one. In this logical conundrum the reader is left, nettled by interpretive possibilities no gloss can smooth but that serve to keep the game and so the poem alive. The poem's difficulties are, in this sense, both its content and its style, which is as it should be, for such are the ends, and the satisfactions, of Gwendolyn Brooks's craft.

NOTES

1. *Black on White: A Critical Survey of Writing by American Negroes* (1966; rpt. New York: Viking-Compass, 1969), pp. 89, 90.

2. *Singers of Daybreak: Studies in Black American Literature* (Washington: Howard Univ. Press, 1974), p. 43.

3. "The Decline of Anglo-American Poetry," *Virginia Quarterly*, 54 (1978), 74.

4. Other issues are equally at stake, issues extending beyond poetry proper and suggested by remarks such as Littlejohn's contention that Brooks is "far more a poet than a Negro," p. 80, and Dan Jaffe's observation that "the label 'black poetry' cheapens the achievement of Gwendolyn Brooks" ("Gwendolyn Brooks: An Appreciation from the White Suburbs," in *The Black American Writer*, ed. C.W.E. Bigsby [DeLand: Everett/Edwards, 1969], II, 92). On Brooks's poetics and her desire to produce work espousing a black aesthetic, see Norris H. Clark, "Gwendolyn Brooks and a Black Aesthetic," in *A Life Distilled: Gwendolyn Brooks, Her Poetry and Fiction*, ed. Maria K. Mootry and Gary Smith (Urbana: Univ. of Illinois Press, 1987), pp. 81–99; and Clara Claiborne Park, "First Fight, Then Fiddle," *The Nation*, 26 September 1987, pp. 308–12. For Brooks's comments on this matter, see Martha H. Brown and Marilyn Zorn, "GLR Interview: Gwendolyn Brooks," *Great Lakes Review*, 6, No. 1 (1979), 48–55.

5. *Annie Allen* (New York: Harper, 1949), pp. 12–13.

6. Charles Israel, "Gwendolyn Brooks," in *American Poets Since World War II, Part 1: A–K* (*Dictionary of Literary Biography*, Vol. 5), ed. Donald J. Greiner (Detroit: Gale, 1980), p, 101; D.H. Melhem, *Gwendolyn Brooks: Poetry and the Heroic Voice* (Lexington: Univ. Press of Kentucky, 1987), p. 60; and Harry A. Shaw, *Gwendolyn Brooks* (Boston: Twayne, 1980), pp. 71–72, 108–09.

7. As a "note" on Annie's childhood and girlhood, "'Do Not Be Afraid of No'" is not alone in hearing a puzzling relation to the sequence and to the hook as a whole: cf. "'Pygmies Are Pygmies Still, Though Percht on Alps,'" *Annie Allen*, p. 14.

8. "Gwendolyn Brooks' Poetic Realism: A Developmental Survey," in *Black Women Writers (1950–1980): A Crucial Evaluation*, ed. Mari Evans (New York: Doubleday, 1984), p. 92. Kent's observation is echoed elsewhere: see Blyden Jackson and Louis D. Rubin, Jr., *Black Poetry in America* (Baton Rouge: Louisiana State Univ. Press, 1974), pp. 81–85; Jackson and Rubin argue, with particular reference to *Annie Allen*, that Brooks's method is constantly to subordinate matters of sex or race to universal insights.

9. "Gwendolyn Brooks's *A Street in Bronzeville*, the Harlem Renaissance and the Mythologies of Black Women," *MELUS*, 10, No. 5 (1983), 55.

10. Park, "Fight First, Then Fiddle," p. 308.

11. "One Big Interview," in *Picked-Up Pieces* (Greenwich, Conn.: Fawcett, 1975), p. 485.

12. *American Heritage Dictionary*, New College Ed., 1979.

13. On the reasons why both "yes" and the easy "no" make for poor art, see Leslie Fiedler, "No! In Thunder," in *No! In Thunder* (Boston: Beacon, 1960), pp. 1–18.

14. Letter to Nathaniel Hawthorne, 16 (?) April 1851, in *The Portable Melville*, ed. Jay Leyda (New York: Viking, 1952), p. 428.

15. "Fight First, Then Fiddle," pp. 311, 310.

16. This assessment is admittedly a matter of personal taste. Brooks herself is clearly—and particularly after 1967—not averse to writing just such poetry, as *In the Mecca* and critical favorites such as "We Real Cool" indicate. Again, I would direct the interested reader to Park, Clark, and Brown and Zorn.

HENRY TAYLOR

Gwendolyn Brooks: An Essential Sanity

Gwendolyn Brooks's emergence as an important poet has been less schematic, but not less impressive, than commentary upon it has suggested. It is difficult to isolate the poems themselves from the variety of reactions to them; these have been governed as much by prevailing or individual attitudes toward issues of race, class, and gender, as by serious attempts at dispassionate examination and evaluation. Furthermore, Brooks's activities in behalf of younger writers have demonstrated her generosity and largeness of spirit, and wide recognition of these qualities has led some critics away from the controlled but genuine anger in many of the poems. Brooks has contributed to this process; in interviews, and in her autobiographical *Report from Part One* (1972), she speaks engagingly and with apparent authority about her own work, and many of her judgments have become part of the majority view of her career. Nevertheless, it is worthwhile to consider whether there might be more unity in the body of her work than conventional divisions of her career suggest.

Brooks herself, as William H. Hansell has noted, indicated the divisions when, "in a 1976 interview at the University of Wisconsin–La Crosse, [she] said that her work falls into three periods that correspond to 'changes' in her perspective." Hansell's note: "Works of the first period are *A Street in Bronzeville* (1945), *Annie Allen* (1949) and *The Bean*

Taylor, Henry, "Gwendolyn Brooks: An Essential Sanity." *On Gwendolyn Brooks: Reliant Contemplation*, Stephen Caldwell Wright, ed. 254-275. © by the University of Michigan 1996. Reprinted by permission.

Eaters (1960). The second period is represented by the ."New Poems" section of *Selected Poems* (1963) and by two uncollected poems, 'The Sight of the Horizon' (1963) and 'In the Time of Detachment, in the Time of Cold' (1965). The third phase of her development is marked by her most recent collections: *In the Mecca* (1969) [1968], *Riot* (1969), *Family Pictures* (1970) and *Beckonings* (1975)."[1]

Whether a writer's development involves improvement is highly questionable, but writers often think they are improving, because they are usually more interested in work in progress than they are in work long since completed. Since the mid-1960s, Brooks has revealed these attitudes in numerous comments on her awakening to the situation of the Black writer in America. On the other hand, when she ended her association with Harper & Row, and began to place her work with Black publishers, she retained the rights in her early work, and reprinted the bulk of it in a collected volume entitled *Blacks*.[2] The stark inclusiveness of that one-word title suggests that Brooks perceives unity as well as variety in the range of her concerns and voices.

Report from Part One and, more recently, the late George Kent's *A Life of Gwendolyn Brooks*,[3] provide generous insight into the origins of Brooks's art. Her own work provides a livelier evocation of her early years than Kent manages in his first two chapters, but he has made a thorough examination of the young girl's notebooks, which she kept industriously. The child appears to have taken seriously her mother's prediction that she would grow up to be the "lady Paul Laurence Dunbar." Kent finds that she was a victim of an intraracial prejudice which put very dark girls at a social disadvantage among Black people of her age. (This theme recurs in Brooks's poetry through *In the Mecca*.) The energy which might have gone into a more active social life was instead poured into poems and stories which show promise more in their profusion than in their accomplishment.

Though she had been publishing poems in the *Chicago Defender* since her high school days, she was twenty-eight when *A Street in Bronzeville* (poems, 1945) appeared. Concerning what was "new" about it, Kent writes:

> The poet had rejected the exotic vein of the Harlem Renaissance—the celebration of unique racial values, such as defiance of social proscription through emphasis upon joy

and soul. A few poems in *A Street* work close to this vein, allowing the reader the enjoyment of the old colorful images, but use one device or another to bring them to the court of critical intelligence. Thus "patent leather" and other poems devalue the "hipness" that the Harlem Renaissance would have celebrated.[4]

As have all American poets, Brooks inherited the old problem of language, which in the nineteenth century divided poets into rebels and loyalists—those who knew that the central problem was to establish independence in the language of the colonizing country, and those who were content with the poetic tradition of the colonizers. This dilemma is exponentially more difficult for a Black woman; a term like "the lady Paul Laurence Dunbar" hardly needs comment on the forms of oppression it implies and, implicitly, accepts.

Still, Brooks had applied herself assiduously to the absorption of a largely white male tradition, in the apparent belief that all great poetry in English had something of value to teach her. *A Street in Bronzeville* introduced a poet of more technical accomplishment than was usual even in the mid-1940s. Forty-five years later, the variety of forms and tones in the collection remains impressive; Donne, Robinson, Frost, Dickinson, and even Ogden Nash seem to have left occasional marks, as well as Hughes and the blues.

But what strikes most forcibly now is the sophistication, and the Dickinsonian way in which sophistication sometimes becomes a shield, from behind which almost invisible darts fly often and accurately. Throughout Brooks's poetry, delicate satire regularly breaks through a surface which is pretending in some way to be well-behaved.

In twelve lines, for example, "the vacant lot" provides a richly populated scene, in tones modulating from apparent nostalgia and regret through sarcasm to controlled, satiric flatness:

Mrs. Coley's three-flat brick
Isn't here any more.
All done with seeing her fat little form
Burst out of the basement door;
And with seeing her African son-in-law
(Rightful heir to the throne)

With his great white strong cold squares of teeth
And his little eyes of stone;
And with seeing the squat fat daughter
Letting in the men
When majesty has gone for the day—
And letting them out again.

(41)

Throughout *A Street*, individual poems have lowercase titles when they are grouped under a larger heading. Despite this consistency, however, the device occasionally creates a local effect; here the suggested insignificance of the lot is emphasized by an immediate and energetic portrayal of what is not there. Among the departures is the mysterious African son-in-law, who briefly dominates the poem, his teeth packing the seventh line with stressed monosyllables, but whose "majesty," by the end of the poem, is cruelly diminished.

The gulf between imagined majesty and hard reality is a frequent theme in *A Street*. Its most ambitious treatment is "The Sundays of Satin-Legs Smith," a narrative of just over 150 lines in which satire is deepened by compassion. The ironic contrasts begin with the title; the protagonist's name yokes the exotic and the ordinary. The polysyllabic opening introduces a narrator whose self-consciously elegant language is mock-heroic:

Inamoratas, with an approbation,
Bestowed his title. Blessed his inclination.

He wakes, unwinds, elaborately: a cat
Tawny, reluctant, royal. He is fat
And fine this morning. Definite. Reimbursed.

(42)

As Satin-Legs commences his morning ablutions, the speaker becomes an ironically patient lecturer, addressing a "you" who is presumed innocent of the life being unfolded here, and who may therefore be taken as white. In the following excerpt, the sentence "Maybe so" ends a passage of fourteen lines, concerning the appropriateness of Satin-Legs's choice of scents and oils, which both recalls and quietly subverts the sonnet tradition:

... might his happiest
Alternative (you muse) be, after all,
A bit of gentle garden in the best
Of taste and straight tradition? Maybe so.
But you forget, or did you ever know,
His heritage of cabbage and pigtails,
Old intimacy with alleys, garbage pails,
Down in the deep (but always beautiful) South
Where roses blush their blithest (it is said)
And sweet magnolias put Chanel to shame.

(42–43)

Satin-Legs has only an artificial flower, made of feathers, for his lapel; in the first of two brief asides, the speaker says, "Ah, there is little hope." Satin-Legs will have "his lotion, lavender, and oil."

Unless you care to set the world a-boil
And do a lot of equalizing things,
Remove a little ermine, say, from kings,
Shake hands with paupers and appoint them men....

(43)

But the speaker decisively returns to an inspection of "The innards of this closet." More strongly than "Maybe so" above, "innards" underscores the speaker's dualistic sense of language and class; if Satin-Legs is being satirized, so is the addressee, whose ignorance is more broadly satirized in such later poems as "I love those little booths at Benvenuti's," "The Lovers of the Poor," and "Bronzeville Woman in a Red Hat."

The closet contains the gaudy accoutrements of such a dandy as Satin-Legs is, or aspires to be; colors are "sarcastic," tailoring is "cocky," ties are "hysterical." Following this exposition of his tastes, two lines in a second brief aside hover between solemnity and humor:

People are so in need, in need of help.
People want so much that they do not know.

(44)

True enough; but the idea is complicated by its placement, which suggests that Satin-Legs needs advice from a refined haberdasher. Creating himself "is all his sculpture and his art." However, after he enters the street, halfway through the poem, there is no further description of his appearance; instead, we see how things appear to him. Through the narrator, we experience his surroundings more vividly than he does. "He hears and does not hear" an alarm clock, children, a plane, voices, and the elevated train. "He sees and does not see" broken windows patched with newspaper, children in worn but decently patched clothes, and

> men estranged
> From music and from wonder and from joy
> But far familiar with the guiding awe
> Of foodlessness.
>
> (45)

The music he hears is popular blues; the narrator notes the absence of strains by Saint-Saëns, Grieg, Tschaikovsky, Brahms, and questions whether he could love them if they were audible; one brings to music what one is:

> The pasts of his ancestors lean against
> Him. Crowd him. Fog out his identity.
> Hundreds of hungers mingle with his own....
>
> (46)

From a movie, where he is reminded that "it is sin for his eye to eat of" the heroine's "ivory and yellow," he proceeds toward the goal of all his efforts. In a line that tumbles anticlimactically from faint echoes of the courtly tradition to a place where main courses are served on meat platters, he "Squires his lady to dinner at Joe's Eats" (46). The "lady" is different every Sunday, but there are constant characteristics, most of them supplied by the overstated dress and makeup that Satin-Legs could be expected to admire. The ending of the poem subtly suggests that this is a kind of death-in-life. Remarking that the food is plentiful at Joe's Eats, the narrator interjects: "(The end is—isn't it?—all that really matters.)" The poem concludes with the achievement of Satin-Legs's objective:

Her body is like new brown bread
Under the Woolworth mignonette.
Her body is a honey bowl
Whose waiting honey is deep and hot.
Her body is like summer earth,
Receptive, soft, and absolute ...

(47)

The slant rhymes undercut the directness of the statements, and draw attention to the "absolute" nature of receptive earth, where, in the old courtly usage, Satin-Legs Smith is about to die. Unlike the pool players in "We Real Cool," who "die soon" in many senses, Satin-Legs will survive; this Don Juan's version of Hell is to repeat this cycle indefinitely, with "little hope" of redemption. The ignorant white observer is presumed to accept this ending as all that really matters.

Brooks wrote this accomplished poem toward the end of her work on *A Street*, probably in response to Richard Wright's evaluation of the manuscript she had sent to Harper & Brothers; he praised her skill and genuineness, but added that "most volumes of poems usually have one really long fine poem around which shorter ones are added or grouped."[5]

A Street concludes with a sequence of twelve sonnets, "Gay Chaps at the Bar," which is close enough to what Wright was asking for. "Gay Chaps" is among the stronger poetic responses we have to World War II, and deserves inclusion in anthologies devoted to that subject, along with "Negro Hero," the monologue of a Black mess attendant who took up a machine gun and used it effectively when his ship was attacked at Pearl Harbor, despite regulations of the strictly segregated Navy of that era, in which Black personnel did not handle firearms.

Brooks adopts several points of view throughout "Gay Chaps at the Bar"—omniscient, first person singular, first person plural—and her speakers demonstrate that Black soldiers suffered the same terrors and hopes as any other soldiers. But she is equally concerned to present the injustices of the Black warriors' situation, and reasonable doubts about what they might have been fighting for. The sonnets submit to convention in several ways, but Brooks uses slant rhyme in them more often than she had earlier; they extend the range of sonic choices, and help to emphasize the paradox that these men were fighting for a country which in many ways refused to claim them.

Brooks's interest in traditional technical virtuosity reaches an apex in *Annie Allen*, the collection for which she received the 1950 Pulitzer Prize. The book is arranged in three sections: "Notes from the Childhood and the Girlhood," "The Anniad" (which includes the long poem of that title and two short pieces as "Appendix to The Anniad"), and "The Womanhood." The eleven short poems in the first section establish Annie as a daydreamer, resentful of restrictions imposed by her parents and society, hopeful of some idealized rescuer.

"The Anniad" is a technical tour de force: 301 lines in forty-three seven-line stanzas, employing thirty different rhyme schemes, a compelling meter (trochaic tetrameter catalectic), and a diction that is elaborate, dense, and compressed. Paraphrase is often difficult, and it is also difficult to resist being carried along on the sound waves, heedless of incomprehension. There is a definite narrative; some of the details are obscure, though the poems in the first section of *Annie Allen* provide background for the entrance to the poem:

> Think of sweet and chocolate,
> Left to folly or to fate,
> Whom the higher gods forgot,
> Whom the lower gods berate;
> Physical and underfed
> Fancying on the featherbed
> What was never and is not.
>
> What is ever and is not.
> Pretty tatters blue and red,
> Buxom berries beyond rot,
> Western clouds and quarter-stars,
> Fairy-sweet of old guitars
> Littering the little head
> Light upon the featherbed.
> . . . .
> Watching for the paladin
> Which no woman ever had,
> Paradisiacal and sad
> With a dimple in his chin
> And the mountains in the mind;

Ruralist and rather bad,
Cosmopolitan and kind.

(99–100)

The imperative of the first line, repeated six more times throughout the poem, implies a reader or listener. This strategy, not as fully developed as in "The Sundays of Satin-Legs Smith," still gives the speaker awareness of an audience, and an inclination to perform. In various tones—affectionate tolerance, adult amusement, or sadness and anger—the speaker shows us the impossible romantic aspirations that fill Annie's "light" and "little" head. The paladin's virtues are impossibly contradictory; that he is not a person, but an imaginary being, is obvious enough, but emphasis is provided in the relative pronoun: "Which no woman ever had."

As she grows older, a "man of tan" courts Annie, and his qualities and her predilections arouse her:

What a hot theopathy
Roisters through her, gnaws the walls,
And consumes her where she falls
In her gilt humility.

(100)

They move to a "lowly room" which she tries to transform into a lovely love nest. There follows a passage which has been subject to more than one critical bias:

Doomer, though, crescendo-comes
Prophesying hecatombs.
Surrealist and cynical.
Garrulous and guttural.
Spits upon the silver leaves.
Denigrates the dainty eves
Dear dexterity achieves.

Names him. Tames him. Takes him off,
Throws to columns row on row.
Where he makes the rifles cough,

Stutter. Where the reveille
Is staccato majesty.
Then to marches. Then to know
The hunched hells across the sea.

Vaunting hands are now devoid.
Hieroglyphics of her eyes
Blink upon a paradise
Paralyzed and paranoid.
But idea and body too
Clamor "Skirmishes can do.
Then he will come back to you."

                                        (101–102)

To the reader biased toward a belief in the occasional usefulness of
paraphrase, "roomer" presents difficulties; but the second of these three
stanzas helps to identify it as a power suggestive of Uncle Sam, the draft,
and the intrusion of war. Noisily, prophesying slaughter, speaking almost
bestially, it attacks the little home life Annie has with difficulty achieved.
It calls "tan man's" name, inducts him into armed service, sets him to
drill with guns, reveille, and marches, and ships him overseas. Annie,
bereft, looks blankly on her altered life, but wants to believe he will not
be killed.

Hortense J. Spillers, on the other hand, offers a feminist reading of
the passage in "Gwendolyn the Terrible: Propositions on Eleven
Poems": "As it turns out, he is not the hot lover 'theopathy' would make
him out to be, but Annie denies it, fearing that to say so would be to
evoke an already imminent betrayal: [quotes first and third of above
stanzas]. This scene of 'win,' brought on by sexual impotence, gains a
dimension of pathos because it anticipates the woman's ultimate
loneliness, but this judgment is undercut by the caricature of the male."[6]

This may constitute misreading for the sake of an overriding
theme, but Spillers characterizes, with justice and unintended irony, the
poem's "specific end: to expose the sadness and comedy of self-delusion
in an equally deluded world."[7]

Upon his return, troubled by conflicting recollections of horror
and of power, and by predilections imposed on him in a white-
dominated society, "tan man" finds a mistress whose color is more honey

than chocolate. The twenty-third stanza begins by repeating the first line of the poem, and launches an account of Annie's life alone, from winter through the following fall; she attempts social gaiety, esoteric learning, the high life, and then tries to settle toward her husband's return. The speaker turns to "tan man" and chastises him:

> Hence from scenic bacchanal,
> Preshrunk and droll prodigal!
> Smallness that you had to spend,
> Spent. Wench, whiskey and tail-end
> Of your overseas disease
> Rot and rout you by degrees.
>
> (107)

At home again, he wastes away, and at last leaves the world, and the two women, who are contrasted harshly in successive stanzas:

> Leaves his mistress to dismiss
> Memories of his kick and kiss,
> Grant her lips another smear,
> Adjust the posies at her ear,
> Quaff an extra pint of beer,
> Cross her legs upon the stool,
> Slit her eyes and find her fool.
>
> Leaves his devotee to bear
> Weight of passing by his chair
> And his tavern. Telephone
> Hoists her stomach to the air.
> Who is starch or who is stone
> Washes coffee-cups and hair,
> Sweeps, determines what to wear.
>
> (108–109)

The second of these stanzas, the fortieth in the poem, reflects Annie's static helplessness; it is the only one with two rhymes instead of three. She becomes the victim of nightmares and a harried resignation, but the final stanza mutes the verbal flash:

Think of almost thoroughly
Derelict and dim and done.
Stroking swallows from the sweat.
Fingering faint violet.
Hugging old and Sunday sun.
Kissing in her kitchenette
The minuets of memory.

                                                    (109)

Though much of the satire in this poem seems to be directed at Annie's innocent romanticism, and at the circumstances which have nourished it, the tone of the last stanza turns toward sympathy. Annie's pathetic stillness, the amatory participles describing small aimless gestures, are mitigated by the "almost" in the first line, and by the iambic fullness of the last. Annie is now twenty-four, and has endured a series of disillusionments and bereavements. If she is to blame for some of them, so is the world.

Whereas the poems of the first two sections of *Annie Allen* speak of Annie in the third person, the third section opens with a sequence of five sonnets, "the children of the poor," in which the mother speaks in the first person. The sequence quickly ranges over several questions arising from the profoundly mixed blessings and curses of disadvantaged parenthood—how to protect children, teach them, prepare them for the fact of death. The fourth sonnet is a complex variation on the persistent American theme that art could not flourish in the period when people of ability were occupied with settling the country. Its punctilious adherence to Petrarchan conventions of structure momentarily withholds the sarcasm that bursts through in the sestet. It begins with two short sentences occupying exactly half a line: "First flight. Then fiddle." The remainder of the octave describes the fiddling, fraught with "feathery sorcery" and "silks and honey," yet covertly rebellious:

                muzzle the note
With hurting love; the music that they wrote
Bewitch, bewilder.

The sestet returns to the fighting:

But first to arms, to armor. Carry hate
In front of you and harmony behind.
Be deaf to music and to beauty blind.
Win war. Rise bloody, maybe not too late
For having first to civilize a space
Wherein to play your violin with grace.

(118)

Enjambment and shifting caesuras lend energy to much of the poem, but in the final couplet the energy is "civilized" to excessive tameness, reinforcing the "maybe" in the preceding line. The poem hovers between satire and direct polemic, both attacking and appropriating the notion behind it.

The inclusive vision that results in such a poem finds a variety of more single-minded expressions in the remainder of the book; this section of *Annie Allen* contains a few underachieved poems, but on the whole it is a sustained illustration of Brooks's many virtues. There are straightforwardly affectionate sketches, satiric portrayals of Black characters and of ignorant or sheltered whites, seized moments in the manner of Emily Dickinson, love poems, polemical addresses. The book concludes with an untitled poem of considerable power, addressing "Men of careful turns, haters of forks in the road," and declaring the speaker's full humanity. Its characterization of establishment caution is icily exact:

"What
We are to hope is that intelligence
Can sugar up our prejudice with politeness.
Politeness will take care of what needs caring.
For the line is there.
And has a meaning. So our fathers said—
And they were wise—we think—at any rate,
They were older than ourselves. And the report is
What's old is wise. At any rate, the line is
Long and electric. Lean beyond and nod.
Be sprightly. Wave. Extend your hand and teeth.
But never forget it stretches there beneath."

(140)

The poem ends with a chilling recognition that things will not soon change, especially if polite requests are depended on. The last line memorably combines determination and pessimism:

> Let us combine. There are no magics or elves
> Or timely godmothers to guide us. We are lost, must
> Wizard a track through our own screaming weed.
>
> (140)

If there are sharp divisions in Brooks's career, one of them comes at this point. As George Kent puts it, "For both whites and Blacks, Gwendolyn would from now on be tagged 'the first Negro to win a Pulitzer Prize,' and with that label would come the roles of spokeswoman and arbiter in the upper realms of her city's and her nation's cultural affairs" (Kent 102). We may be able to see whether Brooks's work changed noticeably after this, but the question is obfuscated by the churning assortment of critical responses to her new status. The problem of Brooks's place in a white literary establishment had in fact been thrown into relief by Paul Engle's August 26, 1945, review in the *Chicago Tribune*, of *A Street in Bronzeville*. Especially in the 1940s, trying to declare Brooks's transcendence of racial differences was to fall into the nearly inescapable trap of simultaneously affirming and denying the importance of race in her work: "Miss Brooks is the first Negro poet to write wholly out of a deep and imaginative talent, without relying on the fact of color to draw sympathy and interest.... The finest praise that can be given to the book is that it would be a superb volume of poetry in any year by a person of any color."[8]

There is no reason to doubt Engle's sincere admiration of Brooks's work, or the honesty of his conviction that race should not be the issue that it is; but it is hard to get away from the hint of exclusiveness, the suggestion that Brooks is a fine poet, not regardless of her color, but despite it. In later years, increasing numbers of Black writers would question the extent of Brooks's commitment to Blackness; but there were confusing earlier questions by less militant writers. J. Saunders Redding, for example, in a generally favorable review of *Annie Allen* in the *Saturday Review*, found references to intraracial color preferences too esoteric: "Who but another Negro can get the intimate feeling, the racially-particular acceptance and rejection, and the oblique bitterness of this? ... The question is ... whether it is not this penchant for coterie stuff—the special allusions, the highly special feeling derived from an even more special experience—that has brought poetry from the most highly regarded form of communication to the least regarded."9

Redding and Engle were saying remarkably similar things, and missing an important element of Brooks's art. She sought to make her Black characters as rounded as poetry permits; this necessarily involved treating aspects of the Black experience which are imposed by white society. Through her first two books, her anger at injustice is comparatively restrained, but several poems in *The Bean Eaters* greatly increase the pressure of rage against the control of mature technique.

In one or two instances, the pressure overcomes control. "A Bronzeville Mother Loiters in Mississippi. Meanwhile, a Mississippi Mother Burns Bacon" is a daring response to the murder of Emmett Till, a Chicago teenager who was beaten and killed in 1955, during a visit to Mississippi. Brooks adopts the point of view of the young white woman who accused the youth of making sexual advances toward her. The sympathetic portrayal of the woman is striking; the husband, however, is a flat symbol of murderous white male oppression. He deserves that status, but in the poem he fails to earn it; instead of a plausible and therefore frightening and disgusting human, we have something too much like a cartoonist's drawing of Bull Connor. On the other hand, the woman's romantic vision of southern womanhood collapses convincingly before her growing knowledge of the Dark Villain's innocent youth:

> Had *she* been worth the blood, the cramped cries, the little
>   stuttering bravado,
>   The gradual dulling of those Negro eyes,
>   The sudden, overwhelming *little-boyness* in that barn?
>   (336)

Flat portrayal of white characters is more effective in such satirical poems as "The Lovers of the Poor" and "Bronzeville Woman in a Red Hat," where reduction of characters to cartoons serves a dual function: it permits broad sarcasm and indulgence in playful diction, and it invites the white reader to feel excluded from the portrait until it is too late to escape inclusion in it. Both poems portray whites in the act of dehumanizing Blacks, though "Bronzeville Woman" is heavy-handed in this respect. A rich and overbearing woman has had to replace her Irish housemaid, and the agency has sent a Black woman, whom the employer calls "it" throughout the poem. The portrayal becomes more effective, if nearly sentimental, in contrasting the reactions of the employer and the employer's child, "Not wise enough to freeze or be afraid" (370).

The other major treatment of racial violence is "The Ballad of Rudolph Reed," a fiercely ironic narrative of the violence that follows a Black family's purchase of a house in a white neighborhood. Traditional ballad meter and language give the poem a strange atmosphere of remoteness:

> Rudolph Reed was oaken.
> His wife was oaken too.
> And his two good girls and his good little man
> Oakened as they grew.

(376)

Contemporary racist brutality breaks with great force into such a setting, but the poem is strong enough to contain the atrocity of Reed's death, which comes as he is defending his house against rock-throwers who have wounded one of his daughters. The end of the poem is a powerful tableau of grief and strength:

> By the time he had hurt his fourth white man
> Rudolph Reed was dead.
> His neighbors gathered and kicked his corpse.
> "Nigger—" his neighbors said.
>
> Small Mabel whimpered all night long,
> For calling herself the cause.
> Her oak-eyed mother did no thing
> But change the bloody gauze.

(378)

These somewhat extended poems concerned with racial injustice, white insensitivity, and violence, are scattered through an unusually varied collection of shorter poems, from the brilliant miniature "We

Real Cool" to such humorous pieces as "On the Occasion of the Open-Air Formation of the Olde Tymer's Walking and Nature Club." It is this mixture, perhaps, more than the presence of the longer poems, which led some readers to regret the increased emphasis on social issues in *The Bean Eaters*—as if social issues were making their first appearance in Brooks's work. It is true that these longer poems are more explicit, and reveal anger more openly, than do most of Brooks's earlier poems; but most of the shorter poems aroused regret that Brooks could not be consistently polite.

The new poems in *Selected Poems* (1963) did little to change these impressions; "Riders to the Blood-Red Wrath," with its evocations of African majesty, the squalor of slave ships, and the commitment of Freedom Riders, both extends and rejects the polemical manner. Its content is occasion for celebration and exhortation, but in style it reverts to a density Brooks had not used at length since "The Anniad." It crams a racial history into a single consciousness, which ranges without transition between individual and collective recollection, and gathers momentum toward the polemical ending: "To fail, to flourish, to wither or to win. / We lurch, distribute, we extend, begin" (392).

On the other hand, a number of the new poems are brief character sketches; these presage the ambitious and thickly populated *In the Mecca* (1968), the book which has been said to initiate the third period in Brooks's career. If it does mark a significant shift in Brooks's way of writing and of thinking about what she is doing, this is more evident in the shorter poems that follow the title poem. "In the Mecca" is, at just over 800 lines, Brooks's most ambitious single poem; but in strategy and style it is an extension, not a repudiation, of her earlier excellences.

Epigraphs provide the information that the Mecca building, an extravagant apartment complex erected in Chicago in 1891, degenerated into an overcrowded tenement. Kenny J. Williams adds the important fact that the building was razed in 1952.[10]

In bare outline, the narrative is grim: Mrs. Sallie Smith returns to her apartment from hard domestic labor, and begins to prepare dinner for her family of nine children; she notices suddenly that the youngest, Pepita, is missing. There is a fruitless search, police are called, and at last the child is found murdered.

The poem begins with a single line on a page by itself: "Now the way of the Mecca was on this wise." It remains for the poem to unfold the wrathful irony in this echo of Matthew 1:18 ("Now the birth of Jesus Christ was on this wise"). The rest of the poem is based in the present tense; Mrs. Smith encounters four neighbors on the way to her apartment, and each is sketched briefly; Alfred, an English teacher and untalented would-be writer, comes to act as a choral commentator as the poem develops. The children have their distinctive ways of trying to defend themselves against the reality of their lives; Melodie Mary, for example, "likes roaches, / and pities the gray rat." She is dimly aware of headlines announcing strife and suffering in China, but

> What if they drop like the tumbling tears
> of the old and intelligent sky?
> Where are the frantic bulletins
> when other importances die?
> Trapped in his privacy of pain
> the worried rat expires,
> and smashed in the grind of a rapid heel
> last night's roaches lie.
>
> (412)

When the family goes in search of Pepita, they inquire of several neighbors, each of whom is given several lines of characterization. Great-great Gram, who recalls her childhood in slavery, reverts to childhood as she recalls popping little creatures that "creebled" in the dirt of the cabin floor, thus inverting Melodie Mary's treatment of the same subject. Aunt Dill, reveling in her report of a child's rape and murder the previous week, is a gruesome parody of unfeeling self-satisfaction.

Toward the end of this section, there are three portraits without reference to Pepita or her whereabouts. The first, concerning Don Lee, is similar to several other poems Brooks has written about notable Blacks; even in the context of this poem, it appears to portray the poet and activist now named Haki R. Madhubuti. Along with Alfred's references to Léopold Sédar Senghor, "Poet, and muller, President of Senegal," this constitutes unobtrusive anachronism. "In the Mecca" contains few references which can be dated precisely, but some of them, such as Senghor's presidency of Senegal (1960–1980), convey the impression that the Mecca existed in the 1960s. This effect is only slightly complicated for the reader in possession of such arcane as the year of its demolition; the building itself may have been infamous, but its destruction did not significantly change the lives with which the poem is concerned. Brooks's Mecca outlives its namesake, and becomes a perceptible metaphor as well as a symbol.

The increasing desperation of the search for Pepita is reflected in the rapidity with which new characters are introduced from this point on. In the whole poem, over fifty people are mentioned by name or characteristic label; more than half of them appear in the last 200 lines. Because this large cast moves in quickly, sometimes at the rate of four people per line, there is room near the end of the poem for four strophes of between a dozen and two dozen lines each, the first two introducing new characters, the third and fourth returning to Aunt Dill and Alfred, respectively. The two new characters reinforce the balanced vision of the whole poem: Way-Out Morgan is collecting guns, imagining "Death-to-the-Hordes-of-the-White-Men!" (430); Marian is ironing, wishing for some disaster to befall her so she may be noticeable. Absorbed in their visions, they have no time to wonder where Pepita is. Aunt Dill reappears in a gooey cloud of self-satisfaction; the narrator calls her

> the kind of woman you
> peek at in passing and thank your God or zodiac you
> may never have to know
>
> (432)

In this welter of selfishness, Alfred makes a final appearance, allowing Brooks a sly reference to the temporal limbo in which she has erected this cosmos:

> I hate it.
> Yet, murmurs Alfred—
> who is lean at the balcony, leaning—
> something, something in Mecca
> continues to call! Substanceless; yet like mountains,
> like rivers and oceans too; and like trees
> with wind whistling through them. And steadily
> an essential sanity, black and electric,
> builds to a reportage and redemption.

A hot estrangement
A material collapse
that is Construction.

(433)

The next strophe begins with two lines that look back toward this reverie, and forward to the discovery of Pepita's body:

Hateful things sometimes befall the hateful
but the hateful are not rendered lovable thereby.
The murderer of Pepita
looks at the Law unlovably.

(433)

Beneath Jamaican Edward's bed lies the body of Pepita, who "never learned that Black is not beloved." Remembering a rhyme the child once made with "rose," her mother decides to "try for roses." The final four lines of the poem revert to what only Jamaican Edward could have seen, but the powerful image of horror is rendered in a style that can only be the narrator's:

She whose little stomach fought the world had
wriggled, like a robin!
Odd were the little wrigglings
and the chopped chirpings oddly rising.

(433)

"In the Mecca" is a large and largely successful poem, a benchmark in Brooks's career. The poem draws its strength both from her increasing interest in the possibilities for polemic in poetry, and from her broad and deep familiarity with poetry's technical resources. Except in scope and achievement, it is not a radical departure from the work which preceded it. However, it was completed during a time of upheaval in Brooks's sense of herself as a poet, and the shorter poems collected with it are evidence of a major division in Brooks's career.

Much has already been made of the external forces that wrought important changes in Brooks's thinking about her life and work. At the Fisk University Writers' Conference in 1967, she encountered, more forcibly than she had before, the power of young Black writers committed to making a literature for Black people, and to liberating themselves and their people from white oppression. The experience energized her in new ways. She also worked briefly with the Blackstone Rangers, a street gang whose younger mentors, especially Walter Bradford and Don L. Lee, provided encouragement as she sought her "newish voice."[11]

"After Mecca" is a coherent sequence of separate poems; it gathers force by proceeding from individual portraits, through two "public occasion" poems and the three-part "Blackstone Rangers," to "The Sermon on the Warpland" and "The Second Sermon on the Warpland." As the field of vision expands from one poem to the next, the formal scope extends from brief and nearly metrical to more widely various free-verse lines. The diction, however, remains characteristically Brooksian, as in this conclusion to "The Leaders," the second part of "The Blackstone Rangers":

> The Blackstone bitter bureaus
> (bureaucracy is footloose) edit, fuse
> unfashionable damnations and descent;
> and exulting, monstrous hand on monstrous hand,
> construct, strangely, a monstrous pearl or grace.
>
>   (448)

But along with certainty that she had much to learn from younger Black writers, there came a desire to reach audiences unaccustomed to hearing or reading poetry. This arose partly from increasing doubt about dependence on the Eurocentric tradition she had so thoroughly commanded for most of her career; at this point, the language problem referred to early in this essay becomes extremely difficult, despite Anglo-American's flexibility and relative openness to other traditions. With a few notable exceptions such as "We Real Cool," Brooks's poetry has depended not only on fresh and unusual language, but on the varying degrees of surface difficulty that such wordplay often creates. Her attempts at a more accessible style have sometimes resulted in oversimplified moralizing, and in indecision about which poems or versions of poems to reprint.

Of the roughly fifty poems Brooks published between 1968 and

1987, a few have appeared only in periodicals, and only nineteen are collected in *Blacks*. A white reader might be tempted to think that some of this indecision arises from Brooks's having accepted, in 1985, her second major accolade from the literary establishment, when she became Poetry Consultant to the Library of Congress; but in interviews over the past twenty years, and in her tireless work for Black writers during her tenure at the Library, she has demonstrated unwavering commitment to the cause of freedom for oppressed people.

Brooks's wavering over certain poems is evidence of crisis, but it is important to remember that crisis is usually much more rewarding for artists than for politicians. In adjusting her accustomed tools to her new tasks, she has taken some directions which she seems later to have reconsidered, but occasional frustrations have not sent her back to techniques in which she has long been adept. Her most recent collection, *Gottschalk and the Grande Tarantelle* (Chicago: The David Company, 1988), is cause for gratitude that she has not retreated from trying to perfect her new ways of working.

This handsome chapbook contains only four poems, but one of them is "Winnie," some 375 lines spoken by Winnie Mandela. The character is of course a literary creation, partaking of what Brooks knows of Mrs. Mandela, and of what she knows of herself and the world. There are passages where one might wish that more memorable language had been found for the urgent messages:

> we are all vulnerable—
> the midget, the Mighty,
> the richest, the poor.

> (18)

But Brooks has hold of something here. In her early work, personal history (not necessarily her own) was a dependable provider of material. She began to merge social and political history with that strain in poems like "The Ballad of Rudolph Reed" and "A Bronzeville Mother Loiters," and perfected that merging in "In the Mecca." Now, she is after larger historical scope, and appears to be on the brink of finding the means to achieve it without surrendering particularity. As she has Winnie Mandela say,

This is the time for Big Poems,
roaring up out of sleaze,
poems from ice, from vomit, and from tainted blood.

(19)

NOTES

1. "The Poet-Militant and Foreshadowings of a Black Mystique: Poems in the Second Period of Gwendolyn Brooks." Maria K. Mootry and Gary Smith, A I if e Distilled: Gwendolyn Brooks, Her Poetry and Fiction (U of Illinois P, 1987; hereafter referred to as "Mootry and Smith"), 71 and note, 80.

2. *Blacks* (Chicago: The David Company, 1987; page references following quotations are to this volume unless otherwise specified).

3. George Kent, *A Life of Gwendolyn Brooks* (University Press of Kentucky, 1990). Hereafter referred to as "Kent."

4. Kent, p. 66.

5. Kent, p. 63.

6. Mootry and Smith, p. 230.

7. Ibid., p. 231.

8. Quoted in Kent, pp. 74–75.

9. Ibid., p. 79.

10. Mootry and Smith, p. 60.

11. Kent, pg. 180ff.

HAKI R. MADHUBUTI

Gwendolyn Brooks: Beyond the Wordmaker—
The Making of an African Poet

"There is indeed a new black today. He is different from any the world has
known. He's a tall-walker. Almost firm. By many of his own *brothers* he is
not understood. And he is understood by no white. Not the wise white;
not the schooled white; not the kind white. Your *least* pre-requisite toward
an understanding of the new black is an exceptional Doctorate which can
be conferred only upon those with the proper properties of bitter birth
and intrinsic sorrow. I know this is infuriating, especially to those
professional Negro-understanders, some of them *very* kind, with special
portfolio, special savvy. But I cannot say anything other, because nothing
other is the truth." These words, this precise utterance is Gwendolyn
Brooks 1972, is Gwendolyn Brooks post-1967, a quiet force cutting
through the real dirt with new and energetic words of uncompromising
richness that are to many people unexpected, but welcomed by millions.

When you view Gwendolyn Brooks's work in the pre-1967 period,
you see a poet, a black poet in the actual, (though still actively searching
for her own definitions of blackness) on the roadway to becoming a
conscious African poet or better yet a conscious African woman in
America who chose poetry as her major craft. However, Gwendolyn
Brooks describes her poetry prior to 1967 as "work that was conditioned
to the times and the people." In other words, poetry that leaped from the

Madhubuti, Haki R. "Gwendolyn Brooks: Beyond the Wordmaker—The Making of an
African Poet." *Gwendolyn Brooks' Maud Martha: A Critical Collection.* pp. 81–96. © 2002 by
Jacqueline Bryant. Published by Third World Press. Originally published as the preface to
Report From One (1972). Reprinted by permission.

pages bringing forth ideas, definitions, images, reflections, forms, colors, etc., that were molded over a distance of many years—her poetry notebook started at the age of eleven—as a result of and as a reaction to the American reality. And for black people, regardless of the level of their perception of the world, the American reality has always been a battle, a real alley fight.

The early years reaped with self-awareness—there is no denying this—even though at times the force of her poetic song is strained in iambic pentameter, European sonnets and English ballads. Conditioned! There is a stronger sense of self-awareness than most of her contemporaries with the possible exception of Margaret Walker. She was able to pull through the old leftism of the 1930s and 1940s and concentrate on herself, her people and most of all her "writing." Conditioned! Her definitions of the world as represented in the early poetry are often limited to accommodating her work and her person to definitions that were imposed on her from the outside; and she becomes the reactor rather than the actor. She is being defined by her surroundings and by the environment that has been built around her, but the definitions and poetic direction from the Euro-American world are also much a part of her make-up. As early as 1945 in the book *A Street in Bronzeville*, we see images of womanhood, manhood, justice and race worked into memorable lines: "Abortions will not let you forget. / You remember the children you got that you did not get"; and "Men hep, and cats, or corny to the jive. / Being seen Everywhere (Keeping Alive), / Rhumboogie (and the joint is jumpin', Joe, / Brass Rail, Keyhole, De Lisa, Cabin Inn. / And all the other garbage cans."; and "I had to kick their law into their teeth in order to save them."; and "He was born in Alabama. / He was bred in Illinois. / He was nothing but a / Plain black boy"; and "Mae Belle Jackson's husband / Whipped her good last night. / Her landlady told my ma they had / A knock-down-drag-out fight."; and "Mama was singing / At the midnight Club. / And the place was red / With blues. / She could shake her body / Across the floor / For what did she have / To lose?"; and "you paid for your dinner, Sammy boy, / And you didn't pay with money. / You paid with your hide and my heart, Sammy boy, / For your taste of pink and white honey." As the quoted lines indicate Gwendolyn Brooks is deeply involved with black life, black pain and black spirits. To seek white honey was natural; to seek anything white in those early years was only keeping within the expected, within the encouraged. However, this thing of doing the expected cannot be fully applied to Gwendolyn Brooks because the medium she worked in was that of the unexpected—"Negroes 'just don't write, especially not poetry.'" Her movement into poetry is a profound comment on her self-confidence and speaks to the poetic-vision she possessed. The fact that she chose to be a poet denotes that her view of the "whirlwind" was serious and challenging—yet conditioned.

Her growth and development partially depended upon the climate of the time. Those critical years of the 1930s and 1940s left deep scars of hunger and poverty, but because of a strong and closely knit family, she survived. She has always had unusual encouragement from her mother, who to this day is still quite active in "watching over" her daughter's output. Other major influences varied from Europe's war number two (known as World War II) to the work of Langston Hughes and Richard Wright; the South Side of Chicago where she lived and still lives today, Inez Cunningham Stark at the Southside Community Art Center (Gwendolyn Brooks walked off with four poetry prizes between 1943 and 1945 at Midwestern Writers' Conferences at Northwestern University), the appearance of poems in the *Chicago Defender* and *Poetry* magazine, working with the NAACP's young people's group, appearance in *Mademoiselle* magazine as one of the "Ten Women of the Year" in 1945, grants from the American Academy of Arts and Letters and Guggenheim Fellowships and other publishing in major magazines that published "American" poetry. Gwendolyn Brooks at this time, the late 1940s, was concerned with the "universal fact."

Her work like that of the late Langston Hughes has always touched at some level on the problems of blacks in America. Even allowing that, she was often singled out as the "exception" and proclaimed as an "artist"—a poet of the first rank—a poet who happens to be black; not that Gwendolyn Brooks readily accepted these nebulous titles. There was little she could do about it. We must note that she received major encouragement from all quarters to accept, participate and to be grateful for whatever recognition she received. After all, this was what everybody was working for, wasn't it? To go unnoticed is bad enough, but to go unnoticed and not eat is not a stimulus for creativity. By 1945 she had not only married, but had a son. Her family shared most of the time that was normally used for writing and these few literary "breaks" were not only needed, but well received and actively sought after.

If *A Street in Bronzeville* paved the way, *Annie Allen* opened the door. *Annie Allen* (1949) *ran* away with the Pulitzer Prize—the first black person to be so "honored." After winning the Pulitzer, she *now belonged to everybody*. In the eyes of white poetry lovers and white book promoters, the publicity was to read "she is a poet who happens to be black"; in other words, we can't completely forget her "negroness," so let's make it secondary. Her winning the Pulitzer Prize in 1950 is significant for a number of reasons other than her being the first person of African descent to do so. One unstated fact is obvious; *she was the best poet, black or white, writing in the country at the time.* Also in winning the Pulitzer she became internationally known and achieved a following from her own people whereas normally she would not have had access to them. She attracted those "negro" blacks who didn't believe that one is legitimate unless one is sanctioned by whites first. The Pulitzer did this. It also aided her in the pursuit of other avenues of expression and gave her a foothold into earning desperately needed money by writing reviews and articles for major white publications.

In her continuing frame of reference, the confusion over social responsibility and "art for art's sake" intensified. Even though she didn't actually see herself in the context of Euro-American poetry, she was being defined in that context. She was always the American poet who happened to be Negro—the definition was always from the *negative* to the *positive*. Again a Euro-American definition; again conditioned to accept the contradictory and the dangerous. If you cannot definitely and positively define yourself in accordance with your historical and cultural traditions, how in the world can you be consciously consistent in the direction your person and your work must take in accordance with that which is ultimately best and natural for you? At this time Gwendolyn Brooks didn't think of herself as an African or as an African-American. At best she was a "new negro" becoming black. Her view of history and struggle was that of the traditional American history and had not been challenged by anyone of black substance. In her next book the focus was not on history or tradition, but poetic style.

Annie Allen (1949), important? Yes. Read by blacks? No. *Annie Allen* more so than *A Street in Bronzeville* seems to have been written for whites. For instance, "The Anniad" requires unusual concentrated study. She invents the sonnet-ballad in part 3 of the poem "Appendix to the Anniad, leaves from a loose-leaf war diary." This poem is probably earth-shaking to some, but leaves me completely dry. The poem is characterized by fourteen lines with a three part alternating rhyme scheme and couplet at the last two lines. Only when she talks of "the children of the poor" do we begin to sense the feel of home again: "What shall I give my children? who are poor / Who are adjudged the leastwise of the land" or "First fight. Then fiddle" or "Not that success, for him, is sure, infallible. / But never has he been afraid to reach. / His lesions are legion." In the poem "Truth" we sense that that is what she is about: "And if sun comes / How shall we greet him? / Shall we not dread him, / Shall we not fear him / After so lengthy a / Session with shade? ... Sweet is it, sweet is it / To sleep in the coolness / Of snug unawareness. / The dark hangs heavily / Over the eyes." The book has a very heavy moral tone, a pleading tone and "God's actual" in one way or another is prevalent throughout. The poems range from the ridiculous such as "old laughter" (written when she was nineteen years old) but included in the book:

> The men and women long ago
> In Africa, in Africa,
> Knew all there was of joy to know.
> In sunny Africa
> The spices flew from tree to tree.
> The spices trifled in the air
> That carelessly
> Fondled the twisted hair.
>
> The men and women richly sang
> In land of gold and green and red.
> The bells of merriment richly rang.
>
> But richness is long dead,
> Old laughter chilled, old music done
> In bright, bewildered Africa.
>
> The bamboo and the cinnamon
> Are sad in Africa.

to the careful profundity of "intermission" part 3:

> Stand off, daughter of the dusk,
> And do not wince when the bronzy lads
> Hurry to cream-yellow shining.
> It is plausible. The sun is a lode.
> True, there is silver under
> The veils of the darkness.
> But few care to dig in the night
> For the possible treasure of stars.

But for me there is too much "Grant me that I am human, that I hurt, that I can cry." There is an overabundance of the special appeal to the intelligence of the world-runners, even though paradoxically in part 15 of "the children of the poor," she accurately notes that their special appeal to the "intelligence" has been the argument given to us ever since they raped us from Africa: "What we are to hope is that intelligence / Can sugar up our prejudice with politeness. / Politeness will take care of what needs caring." Yet, Gwendolyn Brooks knows that politeness is not possessed by the enemies of the sun, politeness does not seek to control the world; and their intelligence is as misguided as their need to manipulate every living element that they come in contact with. *Annie Allen* is an important book. Gwendolyn Brooks's ability to use their language while using their ground rules explicitly shows that she far surpasses the best European-Americans had to offer. There is no doubt here. But in doing so, she suffers by not communicating with the masses of black people.

Her work in the late 1950s and early 1960s like that of James Baldwin and Ralph Ellison appealed to a wide cross-section. The mood of the land was integration. Come melt with us in the wind at that time. Some of us are still recovering from the burns. LeRoi Jones (now Imamu Amiri Baraka), William Melvin Kelly, John O. Killens, Conrad Kent Rivers, Mari Evans and Melvin B. Tolson's tone of persuasion was projected toward the conscience of America. They wrote as if America (or the rulers of America) had a conscience or a higher God that it answered to. They felt that America had a moral obligation to its other inhabitants, those who were not *fortunate* enough to be born white and Protestant. However, a close reading of Indian history in America or their own history in America would have wiped those illusions out completely. But, even then the "I'm a writer, not a black writer" madness was in the air and along with it existed other distortions and temptations that forever kept the writers from dealing with their African or African-American perspective. They all produced important works and all, with the possible exception of Ralph Ellison (Melvin B. Tolson and Conrad Kent Rivers are deceased) had their hands on the stop sign and were getting ready to cross the continent into the 1960s. The 1960s for Gwendolyn Brooks was to be an entrance into a new life; however it didn't start with *The Bean Eaters*.

The Bean Eaters (1960) was the major appeal, the quiet confirmation of the "Negro" as an equal. She failed to question the measuring rod. Equal to what? The poems that come alive are the very personal, such as, "In Honor of David Anderson Brooks, My Father" and the title poem "The Bean Eaters." There is much black womanness in this book. Gwendolyn Brooks is careful to give black women their due, long before the women liberationists of the 1970s. Those poems that stick out are, "A Bronzeville Mother Loiters in Mississippi. Meanwhile, a Mississippi Mother Burns Bacon," "The Last Quatrain of the Ballad of Emmett Till," "Mrs. Small," "Jessie Mitchell's Mother," "Bronzeville Woman in a Red Hat" and "Callie Ford."

The power poem is "We Real Cool," of which she says "the ending WE's in 'We Real Cool' are tiny, wispy, weakly argumentative 'Kilroy-is-here' announcements. The boys have no accented sense of themselves, yet they are aware of a semi-defined personal importance. Say the 'we' softly."

The poem "The *Chicago Defender* Sends a Man to Little Rock" is structurally tight and was socially ahead of its time, but in the final analysis again its major appeal is to morality. The last line weakens the poem with "The loveliest lynchee was our Lord." In "A Man of the Middle Class" she shows accurate vision; her criticism of the middle class may be due to the fact that she, in her personal life, refused to become a part of make-up and costumery and insists that those who take part in it are "ineffectual." She also adds, "Moreover, the 'eminent' ones, the eminent successes of the society, whose rules and styles he imitated, seem no more in possession of the answers than he; excellent examples of dimness, moral softness and confusion, they are shooting themselves and jumping out of windows." "The Ballad of Rudolph Reed" is the excursion of a black man and his family into an all-white neighborhood. By moving in he jeopardizes the life of himself (which he loses) and that of his family. The poem shows the black man's will to "better" himself regardless of the sacrifices.

Yet, that type of sacrifice is senseless and unforgivable, and could have been avoided if blacks at that time accurately assessed their enemies. *The Bean Eaters* is to be the last book of this type. There won't be any completely new book of poetry published until *In the Mecca*, and *In the Mecca* "blacked" its way out of the National Book Award in 1968.

"I—who have 'gone the gamut' from an almost angry rejection of my dark skin by some of my brainwashed brothers and sisters to a surprised queenhood in the new black sun—am qualified to enter at least the kindergarten of new consciousness now. New consciousness and trudge-toward-progress." With these words Gwendolyn Brooks begins to actively seek and express a new awareness, a black consciousness. She gives greater insight into her newness when she says: "It frightens me to realize that, if I had died before the age of fifty, I would have died a 'Negro' fraction." This is the beginning of defining from one's own perspective; this perspective is what Gwendolyn Brooks would wrestle with between *The Bean Eaters* and the publication of *In the Mecca*.

Her major associations during this period of redefinition were the young and the "Black" writing that was part of their makeup. She, at first hand, witnessed a resurgence of what has been termed the Black Arts Movement. In every aspect of the creative act, young brothers and sisters began to call their own images, from drama to poetry, from fiction to nonfiction, from plastic arts to film, and so on. In every area of creativity black poets cleaned house and carved their own statues into what they wanted themselves to be, regardless of who was watching and with even less regard for what critics, white and black, said. She felt the deep void when Medgar Evers and Malcolm X left us.

She conducted writers' workshops with the Blackstone Rangers and other young people. She took part in neighborhood cultural events like the dedication of the Organization of Black American Culture's Wall of Respect. She lived through the rebellion in Chicago after King's death while listening with disbelief to Mayor Daley's "Shoot to Kill" orders. She lives four blocks from the Black People's Topographical Center in Chicago, the first in the nation. The murder of Mark Clark and Fred Hampton and of other blacks continued to raise questions in her mind.

And the major questions were: 'What part do I play?,' 'Where do I fit in?,' 'What can I do?' Her first and most important contribution was to be the redirecting of her voice to her people—*first and foremost*. This is what is evident in *In the Mecca*, *Riot*, and *Family Pictures*. She becomes "new music screaming in the sun."

Gwendolyn Brooks's post-1967 poetry is fat-less. Her new work resembles a man getting off meat, turning to a vegetarian diet. What one immediately notices is that all the excess weight is quickly lost. Her work becomes extremely streamlined and to the point. There are still a few excesses with language in *In the Mecca*, but she begins to experiment more with free and blank verse, yet her hand still controlled and timed. *In the Mecca* is about black life in an old Chicago landmark. This was to be her epic of black humanity. She wanted to exhibit all its murders, loves, loneliness, hates, jealousies. "Hope occurred, and charity, sainthood, glory, shame, despair, fear, altruism. Theft, material and moral." She included all the tools of her trade, blank verse, prose verse, off-rhyme, random rhyme, long-swinging free verse, the couplet, the sonnet and the ballad. She succeeds admirably with glimpses of greatness. Let's look at "Way-out Morgan":

> Way-out Morgan is collecting guns
> in a tiny fourth-floor room.
> He is not hungry, ever, though sinfully lean.
> He flourishes, ever, on porridge or pat of bean
> pudding or wiener soup—fills fearsomely
> on visions of Death-to-the-Hordes-of-the-White-Men!
> Death!
> (This is the Maxim painted in big black
> above a bed bought at a Champlain rummage sale.)
> Remembering three local-and-legal beatings, he
> rubs his hands in glee,
> does Way-out Morgan. Remembering his Sister
> mob-raped in Mississippi, Way-out Morgan
> smacks sweet his lips and adds another gun
> and listens to Blackness stern and blunt and beautiful,
> organ-rich Blackness telling a terrible story.
> Way-out Morgan
> predicts the Day of Debt-pay shall begin,

the Day of Demon-diamond,
of blood in mouths and body-mouths,
of flesh-rip in the Forum of Justice at last!
Remembering mates in the Mississippi River,
mates with black bodies once majestic, Way-out
postpones a yellow woman in his bed, postpones
wetnesses and little cries and stomachings—
to consider Ruin.

And there is compassion in "a little woman lies in dust with
roaches. / She never went to kindergarten. / She never learned that black
is not beloved." In "After Mecca" her power continues with the ultimate
in manhood as in "Malcolm X":

Original.
Ragged-round.
Rich-robust.
He had the hawk-man's eyes.
We gasped. We saw the maleness.
The maleness raking out and making guttural the air
and pushing us to walls.

The section on the Blackstone Rangers is outstanding. Look at "As
Seen by Disciplines." "There they are. / Thirty at the corner. / Black,
raw, ready. / Sores in the city / that do not want to heal." Gwendolyn
Brooks knew in her new sense of sophistication and black association
that it was difficult for the sores to heal because of the lukewarm
medication. In "The Leaders" she said that "their country is a Nation on
no map," and challenged, in "The Sermon on the Warpland," "My
people, black and black, revile the River. / Say that the River turns, and
turn the River." In "The Second Sermon on the Warpland," she
commands, "Live and go out. / Define and / medicate the whirlwind."
She ends the book with "Big Bessie":

The time
cracks into furious flower. Lifts its face
all unashamed. And sways in wicked grace.
Whose half-black hands assemble oranges

is tom-tom hearted
(goes in bearing oranges and boom).
And there are bells for orphans—
and red and shriek and sheen.
A garbageman is dignified
as any diplomat.
Big Bessie's feet hurt like nobody's business,
but she stands—bigly—under the unruly scrutiny, stands in the
wild weed.

In the wild weed
she is a citizen,
and in a moment of highest quality; admirable.

It is lonesome, yes. For we are the last of the loud.
Nevertheless, live.

Conduct your blooming in the noise and whip of the
    whirlwind.

The books *Riot* (1969) and *Family Pictures* (1970) are important for
a number of reasons other than the obvious. With the publication of *Riot*
Gwendolyn Brooks began her association with one of the newest and
most significant black publishing companies in the world, Broadside
Press, under the quiet and strong editorship of Dudley Randall. As the
poems in *Riot* and *Family Pictures* will testify, Gwendolyn Brooks was not
only asking critical questions, but seeking substantive answers. She was
very conscious of the contradictions in her own personal life, and as best
as possible—living in a contradictory situation in America—began to
systematically deal with those contradictions.

A major problem was that of Harper and Row publishers, a
company she had been with for twenty-six years. Naturally, she had a
certain affection and dedication to Harper and Row, even though
Harper's never, and I mean that literally, pushed the work of Gwendolyn
Brooks. But the decision that was to be made in regard to Harper's was
not either/or, but: what is best for black people. And, when people begin
to put their lives in a perspective of black people as a body and not as
we've traditionally done—black people as individuals—the power and

influence that we seek will come about because, in the final analysis, the *only* thing that an individual can do individually is *die*. Nobody ever built anything individually.

Thus, Gwendolyn Brooks's movement to Broadside Press was in keeping with what she said in *Family Pictures*: "Blackness / is a going to essences and to unifyings." She became the doer and not just the sayer. She ended her association with Harper and Row with the publication of *The World of Gwendolyn Brooks* and sought out after new boundaries of growth, institution building and black collective association. Before she could enjoy her new comradeship with Broadside Press, other young black writers began leaving Broadside Press and going to large white publishing companies proclaiming—loud and clear—that the "Black Arts Movement was dead" and they had to look after themselves.

Here Gwendolyn Brooks was in her fifties leaving a major white publishing company (and she never accumulated any money or security; she always shared her "wealth") because of her principles and commitment and the new young whom she so admired and patterned herself after were reversing themselves going to where she had just left. This was difficult for her to understand. This would be the black integrity of Gwendolyn Brooks and would lead to her final affirmation of self.

The "death" of the Black Arts Movement as seen by some writers was, of course, only a rationale for their own sick actions, was actually an excuse for the new young "stars" to move from the collective of "we, us and our" to the individuality of "my, me and I," was the excuse used so as not to be held accountable for the madness to come. Let's examine a little closer. The division that resulted is of an elementary nature and is fundamentally important to the writer if he is to remain true to himself and to his work.

The cutting factor was again in the area of definition. How does a black poet (or any black person working creatively) define himself and his work: is he a poet who happens to be black or is he a black man or woman who happens to write? The black and white "art for art's sake" enthusiasts embraced the former and the black nationalists expanded in the latter adding that he is an African in America who expresses himself, his blackness with the written word and that the creativity that he possesses is a gift that should be shared with his people and developed to the highest level humanly possible. And that this "art" form in some way should be used in the liberation of his people.

Gwendolyn Brooks had worked with this same question for about ten years now and had, in her own mind, resolved it. Yet, for the young in whom she had put faith and trust, to reverse themselves made her, too, begin to reexamine her conclusions.

This is the issue. To be able to define one's self from a historically and culturally accurate base and to follow through in your work; keeping the best interest of your history and culture in mind is to—actually—give direction to the coming generations. If one defines one's self as a Russian poet, immediately we know that things that are Russian are important to him and to acknowledge this is not to *leave out the rest of the world* or to limit the poet's range and possibilities in any way.

If a poet defines himself as Chinese we know that that designation carries with it a certain life style which will include Chinese language, dress, cultural mores, feelings, spirituality, music, foods, dance, literature, drama, politics, and so forth. If one is an Indian from India, one is first identified with a *land base*; is identified with a race of people; is identified with all the cultural, religious, and political advantages or disadvantages that are associated with that people whether the "poet" accepts them or not. *This must be understood.* To define one's self is to give direction and this goes without saying, that that direction could either be *positive* or *negative*. When one speaks of a Yasunari Kawabata or a Yukio Mishima, one first through name association links them with Asia (specifically Japan) whether they reside in Asia or not. To speak of Ayi Kwei Armah, Wole Soyinka or David Diop is first to speak of Africa and then the world.

When seeking universality, one always starts with the local and brings to the universal world that which is particularly Russian, Asian, European, Indian, Spanish, African or whatever. If, in 1972, this is not clear I will concede that the "Black Arts Movement" is dead. But the overwhelming evidence shows us that by and large the majority of black "artists" at some level understand their commitment and are educating themselves to the realities of the world more and more: if we don't look after each other, nobody else is supposed to. The black "artist" understands this.

Gwendolyn Brooks is an African poet living and writing in America whose work for the most part has been "conditioned" by her experiences in America. By acknowledging her Africanness, her blackness, she reverses the trend of being defined by the negative to her own definition in the positive. She, in effect, gives direction in her new definition which, if it does nothing else, *forces* her reader to question that definition.

Why does she call herself African? To question our existence in this world critically is the beginning of understanding the world we live in. To begin to understand that we, Africans, in this country constitute the *largest* congregation of African people outside of Africa is important. To understand that black people in this country, who number thirty million upwards, will have to question why we don't have any say—so over domestic policy in reference to ourselves, to question why we have no say-so over foreign policy in relationship to Africa, to question why we exist as other people's door mats is important.

To question is the beginning of empowerment. Why does Gwendolyn Brooks call herself an African? Almost for the same reason that Europeans call themselves Europeans, that Chinese call themselves Chinese, that Russians call themselves Russian, that Americans call themselves Americans—people find a sense of *being*, a sense of worth and substance with being associated with *land*. Associations with final roots gives us not only a history (which did not start and will not end in this country), but proclaims us heirs to a future and it is best when we, while young, find ourselves talking, acting, living and reflecting in accordance with that future which is best understood in the context of the past.

The vision of Gwendolyn Brooks can be seen in lines like:

Say to them,
say to the down-keepers,
the sun-slappers,
the self-soilers,
the harmony-hushers,
"Even if you are not ready for day
it cannot always be night."
You will be right.
For that is the hard home-run.

Live not for Battles Won.
Live not for The-End-of-the-Song.
Live in the along.

The direction Gwendolyn Brooks gives to "Young Afrikans is calm, well thought out and serious:

If there are flowers, flowers
must come out to the road. Rowdy!—
knowing where wheels and people are,
knowing where whips and screams are,
knowing where deaths are, where the kind kills are.

Chester Hines said that "one of the sad things in America is that they try to control the Black people with creativity." And, to control your own creativity is the prerequisite to any kind of freedom or liberation, because if you tell the truth, you don't worry about offending. You just go ahead and cut the ugly away, while building for tomorrow.

We can see in the work of Gwendolyn Brooks of 1972 positive movement from that of the sayer to the doer, where she recognizes that *writing is not enough* for a people in a life and death struggle. For so few black writers to reflect the aspirations and needs of so many (there are about three hundred black writers who are published with any kind of regularity) is a responsibility that should not be taken lightly. Every word has to be considered and worked with so as to use it to its fullest potential. We know that her association with the young had a great effect upon her present work.

Also, her trip to East Africa in 1971 helped to crystallize and finalize her current African association. To understand that Jews' association with Israel is not only cultural, historical and financial, but is necessary for their own survival is to begin to deal with the real world. To understand why the Irish in Chicago sent $25,000 plus to Northern Ireland in 1972 is to associate people with *land* and survival. Gwendolyn Brooks by her dealings with the young poets, Broadside Press and other institutions is only "in keeping" with what other, "European" artists have always done to aid their own. By institutionalizing her thoughts and actions, she is thinking and acting in accordance with a future which will be built by nobody but the people themselves. As in her latest poem, her advice is not confused, clouded, or overly simple, but is the message of tomorrow:

And, boys, in all your Turnings and your Churnings,
remember Afrika.

You have to call your singing and your bringing,
your pulse, your ultimate booming in
the not-so-narrow temples of your Power—
you have to call all that, that is your Poem, AFRIKA.
Although you know
so little of that long leaplanguid land,
our tiny union
is the dwarfmagnificent.
Is the busysimple thing.

See, say, salvage.
Legislate.
Enact our inward law.

Characteristically she has said that

> My aim, in my next future, is to write poems that will
> somehow successfully "call" (see Imamu Baraka's "SOS") all
> black people: black people in taverns, black people in alleys,
> black people in gutters, schools, offices, factories, prisons,
> the consulate; I wish to reach black people in pulpits, black
> people in mines, on farms, on thrones; Not always to
> "teach"—I shall wish often to entertain, to illumine. My
> newish voice will not be an imitation of the contemporary
> young black voice, which I so admire, but an extending
> adaptation of today's Gwendolyn Brooks' voice.

Gwendolyn Brooks is the example for us all, a consistent
monument in the real, unaware of the beauty and strength she has
radiated. Above all, she is the continuing storm that walks with the
English language as lions walk with Africa. Her pressure is above
boiling, cooking new food for our children to grow on.

Chronology

1917	Gwendolyn Brooks is born on June 7 in Topeka, Kansas, to David and Keziah Brooks. One month later the Brooks family moves to Hyde Park, Chicago.
1918	Her brother, Raymond, is born.
1921	The Brooks family moves to Chicago's South Side.
1930	At the age of 13, Brooks's first poem, "Eventide," is published in *American Childhood*.
1932	Brooks enrolls in Hyde Park High School, which was predominately white; she is then transferred to the all black Wendell Phillips High School, and then attends the integrated Englewood High School.
1933	Sends poems to James Weldon Johnson; meets both James Weldon Johnson and Langston Hughes.
1934	Begins weekly contributions to the *Chicago Defender*, a black newspaper, which publishes 75 of her poems in two years; graduates from Englewood High School.
1936	Graduates from Wilson Junior College.
1937	Two poems appear in poetry anthologies.
1939	Marries Henry Lowington Blakely; the couple moves into an apartment on Chicago's South Side.
1940	Her son, Henry Jr., is born on October 10.
1941	Attends Inez Cunningham Stark's poetry workshop at Chicago's South Side Community Art Center.

1943	Wins Midwestern Writers Conference.
1945	First collection of poetry, *A Street in Bronzeville*, is published.
1946–1947	Becomes a Fellow of the American Academy of Arts and Letters and wins a Guggenheim Fellowship both years.
1948	Begins writing book reviews for Chicago newspapers.
1949	Second book of poetry, *Annie Allen*, published, and she is awarded the Pulitzer Prize the following year; she is the first black American to win the Pulitzer.
1951	Her daughter, Nora, is born on September 8.
1953	Publishes *Maud Martha*, a novel. Buys a house.
1956	Publishes *Bronzeville Boys and Girls*, poetry for children.
1959	Her father, David Brooks, dies; she dedicates her third book of poetry to him. The book, *The Bean Eaters*, is published the following year.
1963	*Selected Poems* is published. She accepts her first teaching job at Columbia College, Chicago.
1964	Receives honorary doctorate from Columbia College; this is the first of many honorary degrees from universities across the country.
1967	Experiences political awakening at Fisk University's Black Writers Conference in Nashville, Tennessee.
1968	Book of poetry *In the Mecca* is published; named Poet Laureate of Illinois after Carl Sandburg dies.
1969	Tribute to Brooks, with writers, artists, dancers creating a "Living Anthology." Publishes *Riot* with Broadside Press, a small black publishing house. Separates from husband in November.
1970	Announces she is leaving Harper for Broadside; *Family Pictures* is published; Gwendolyn Brooks Cultural Center opens at Western Illinois University
1971	Publishes *The World of Gwendolyn Brooks*, the last book to be published with Harper; makes pilgrimage to East Africa; *To Gwen with Love* published by admirers;

second children's book, *Aloneness*, is published; Brooks accepts teaching position at City College of New York; after a mild heart attack on Christmas day, she gives up teaching.

1972   Publishes her autobiography, *Report from Part One*.

1973   Reunites with husband; they travel together to France, England, and Ghana.

1974   Publishes children's book, *The Tiger Who Wore White Gloves*.

1975   Publishes her book of poetry *Beckonings*.

1976   Her brother, Raymond, dies.

1978   Her mother, Keziah Brooks, dies.

1980   Starts her own publishing house. Publishes *Primer for Blacks* and *Young Poet's Primer*.

1981   *To Disembark* is published.

1983   Publishes *Very Young Poets*.

1985   She is named Poetry Consultant to the Library of Congress (the U.S. Poet Laureate).

1986   Publishes *The Near-Johannesburg Boy and Other Poems*.

1987   Publishes *The Blacks*, a poetry volume.

1988   Publishes poetry collections *Winnie* and *Gottschalk and the Grande Tarantelle*.

1991   Publishes *Children Coming Home*.

1996   Autobiography *Report from Part Two* published.

2000   Brooks dies at the age of 83 on December 3.

Works By Gwendolyn Brooks

A Street in Bronzeville (1945)

Annie Allen (1949)

Maud Martha (1953)

Bronzeville Boys and Girls (1956)

The Bean Eaters (1960)

Selected Poems (1963)

In the Mecca (1968)

Riot (1969)

Family Pictures (1970)

Aloneness (1971)

The World of Gwendolyn Brooks (1971)

Jump Bad: A New Chicago Anthology (1971) [Editor]

A Broadside Treasury: 1965–1970 (1971) [Editor]

Report from Part One (1972)

The Tiger Who Wore White Gloves, or What You Really Are (1974)

Beckonings (1975)

A Capsule Course in Black Poetry Writing (1975) [with Keorapetse Kgositsile, Haki Madhubuti, and Dudley Randall]

Young Poet's Primer (1980)

Primer for Blacks (1980)

To Disembark (1981)

Mayor Harold Washington and Chicago, the I Will City (1983)

Very Young Poets (1983)

Blacks (1987)

Gottschalk and the Grande Tarantelle (1989)

Winnie (1991)

Children Coming Home (1991)

Report from Part Two (1996)

In Montgomery and Other Poems (2003)

Works about Gwendolyn Brooks

Baker, Houston A., Jr. "The Achievement of Gwendolyn Brooks." *College Language Association Journal* 16 (September 1972): pp. 23–31.

Bigsby, C.W.E.. *The Second Black Renaissance: Essays in Black Literature*, Greenwood Press, 1980.

Bloom, Harold, ed. *Bloom's Major Poets: Gwendolyn Brooks.* Broomall, PA: Chelsea House Press, 2003.

———. *Modern Critical Views: Gwendolyn Brooks.* Philadelphia; Chelsea House Publishers, 2000.

Bolden, B.J. *Urban Rage in Bronzeville: Social Commentary in the Poetry of Gwendolyn Brooks, 1945–1960.* Chicago: Third World Press, 1999.

Brown, Patricia L., Don L. Lee, and Francis Ward, eds. *To Gwen with Love.* Chicago: Johnson, 1971.

Colorado Review (Special Issue) 16, no. 1 (Spring/Summer 1989).

Callahan, John F. "'Essentially an Essential African': Gwendolyn Brooks and the Awakening to Audience." *North Dakota Quarterly* 55, no. 4 (Fall 1987): 59–73.

Christian, Barbara. *Black Feminist Criticism: Perspectives on Black Women Writers.* Elmsford, NY: Pergamon Press, 1985.

Davis, Arthur P. *From the Dark Tower: Afro-American Writers 1900–1960.* Washington, D.C.: Howard University Press, 1974.

Dawson, Emma W. "Vanishing Point: The Rejected Black Woman in the Poetry of Gwendolyn Brooks." *Obsidian II* 4, no. 1 (Spring 1989): pp. 1–11.

Gayle, Addison, Jr. "Gwendolyn Brooks: Poet of the Whirlwind." *Black Women Writers (1950–1980): A Critical Evaluation*. Ed. Mari Evans. Garden City, NY: Anchor Doubleday, 1984. pp. 79–87.

Gayles, Gloria Wade, ed. *Conversations with Gwendolyn Brooks (Literary Conversations)*. University Press of Mississippi, 2003.

Hansell, William H. "The Role of Violence in Recent Poems of Gwendolyn Brooks." *Studies in Black Literature* 5 (Summer 1974): pp. 199–207.

———. "The Uncommon Commonplace in the Early Poems of Gwendolyn Brooks." *College Language Association Journal* 30, no. 3 (1987): pp. 261–77.

Horvath, Brooke K. "The Satisfactions of What's Difficult in Gwendolyn Brook's Poetry." *American Literature* 62, no. 4 (Dec 1990): pp. 606–16.

Hudson, Clenora F. "Racial Themes in the Poetry of Gwendolyn Brooks." *CLA Journal* 17 (September 1973): pp. 16–20.

Hughes, Gertrude R. "Making It Really New: Hilda Doolittle, Gwendolyn Brooks, and the Feminist Potential of Modern Poetry." *American Quarterly* 42 no. 3 (1990): pp. 375–401.

Jimoh, A. Yemisi. "Double Consciousness, Modernism and Womanist Themes in Gwendolyn Brooks's 'The Anniad.'" *MELUS* 23, no. 3 (Fall 1998): pp. 167–87.

Kent, George E. *A Life of Gwendolyn Brooks*. Lexington: University Press of Kentucky, 1990.

Kufrin, Joan. "Gwendolyn Brooks." *Uncommon Women*. Piscataway, N.J.: New Century Publishers, 1981. pp. 35–51.

Lindberg, Kathryne V. "Whose Canon? Gwendolyn Brooks: Founder at the Center of the 'Margins'" in *Gendered Modernisms: American Women Poets and Their Readers*. Eds. Margaret Dickie and Thomas Travisano. Philadelphia: University of Pennsylvania Press, 1996: pp. 283–311.

Loff, Jon N. "Gwendolyn Brooks: A Bibliography." *College Language Association Journal* 17 (1973): pp. 21–32.

Lowney, John. "'A material collapse that is construction': History and Counter-Memory in Gwendolyn Brooks's *In the Mecca*." *MELUS* 23, no.3 (Fall 1998): pp. 3–21.

Madhubuti, Haki R., ed. *Say That the River Turns: The Impact of Gwendolyn Brooks.* Chicago: Third World Press, 1987.

Melhem, D.H. "Gwendolyn Brooks: Humanism and Heroism." In *Heroism in the New Black Poetry: Introductions and Interviews*, 11–38. Lexington: University Press of Kentucky, 1990.

———. *Gwendolyn Brooks: Poetry and the Heroic Voice.* Lexington: University Press of Kentucky, 1987.

Miller, R. Baxter. *Langston Hughes and Gwendolyn Brooks: A Reference Guide.* Boston: G.K. Hall, 1978.

———, ed. "'Define the Whirlwind': Gwendolyn Brooks' Epic Sign for a Generation." *Black American Poets Between Worlds, 1940–1960.* Knoxville: University of Tennessee Press, 1986: pp. 160–73.

Mootry, Maria K., and Gary Smith, eds. *A Life Distilled: Gwendolyn Brooks, Her Poetry and Fiction.* Urbana: University Press of Illinois, 1987.

Shands, Annette O. "Gwendolyn Brooks as Novelist." *Black World* 22, no. 8 (1973): pp. 22–30.

Shaw, Harry B. *Gwendolyn Brooks.* Boston: Twayne, 1980.

Sims, Barbara B. "Brooks's 'We Real Cool.'" *The Explicator* 34, no. 7 (1976): pp. 58.

Smith, Gary. "Gwendolyn Brooks's *A Street in Bronzeville*, the Harlem Renaissance, and the Mythologies of Black Women." *MELUS* 9 (Fall 1983): pp. 33–46.

Tate, Claudia, ed. *Black Women Writers at Work.* New York: Continuum, 1983.

Wright, Stephen Caldwell. *The Chicago Collective: Poems for and Inspired by Gwendolyn Brooks.* Sanford, Florida: Christopher-Burghardt, 1990.

———. *On Gwendolyn Brooks: Reliant Contemplation.* Ann Arbor, Michigan: University of Michigan Press, 1996.

WEBSITES:

http://www.math.buffalo.edu/~sww/brooks/brooks.html
A Gwendolyn Brooks Page

http://www.galegroup.com/free_resources/bhm/bio/brooks_g.htm
Gwendolyn Brooks by Thomson Gale Company

http://www.english.uiuc.edu/maps/poets/a_f/brooks/brooks.htm
Modern American Poetry

http://www.csustan.edu/english/reuben/pal/chap10/brooks.html
PAL: Perspectives in American Literature—A Research
and Reference Guide

Contributors

Harold Bloom is Sterling Professor of the Humanities at Yale University. He is the author of over 20 books, including *Shelley's Mythmaking* (1959), *The Visionary Company* (1961), *Blake's Apocalypse* (1963), *Yeats* (1970), *A Map of Misreading* (1975), *Kabbalah and Criticism* (1975), *Agon: Toward a Theory of Revisionism* (1982), *The American Religion* (1992), *The Western Canon* (1994), and *Omens of Millennium: The Gnosis of Angels, Dreams, and Resurrection* (1996). *The Anxiety of Influence* (1973) sets forth Professor Bloom's provocative theory of the literary relationships between the great writers and their predecessors. His most recent books include *Shakespeare: The Invention of the Human* (1998), a 1998 National Book Award finalist, *How to Read and Why* (2000), *Genius: A Mosaic of One Hundred Exemplary Creative Minds* (2002), and *Hamlet: Poem Unlimited* (2003). In 1999, Professor Bloom received the prestigious American Academy of Arts and Letters Gold Medal for Criticism, and in 2002 he received the Catalonia International Prize.

Amy Sickels is a freelance writer living in New York City. She has published short stories, essays, and book reviews in numerous journals, including *Fourth Genre*, *Kalliope*, and *Literary Review*. She has taught at Pennsylvania State University and holds a B.A. from Ohio University and a Master of Fine Arts in Creative Writing from Pennsylvania State University.

Aimee LaBrie has published stories in journals such as *Beloit Fiction*, *Pleiades*, and *Scribner's Best of the Fiction Workshop* and book reviews in

CALYX and *Willow Springs*. She works as a freelance writer and lecturer in English at Pennsylvania State University and is revising her first novel.

Brooke Kenton Horvath teaches at Kent State University. She has edited several books, including *A Goyen Companion: Appreciation of a Writer's Writer* (1997), *Pynchon and* Mason & Dixon (2000), and *Line Drives: 100 Contemporary Baseball Poems* (2002). She has also contributed articles and chapters to numerous publications, including *American Literature, Modern Fiction Studies*, and *Review of Contemporary Fiction*.

Henry Taylor is a professor of literature and co-director of the M.F.A. program in Creative Writing at American University in Washington, D.C. His collection of poems *The Flying Change* (1985) was awarded the Pulitzer Prize. In addition to his poetry, Taylor has written on other poets in the collection *Compulsory Figures* (1992), and he is highly regarded as a translator.

Haki R. Madhubuti is the director/founder of the Gwendolyn Brooks Center for Black Literature and Creative Writing, and an award-winning poet in his own right. He is Distinguished University Professor/Director of Master of Fine Arts Program in Creative Writing at Chicago State University, and his books include *Black Men: Obsolete, Single, Dangerous?: The African American Family in Transition* (1990), *Claiming Earth: Race, Rage, Rape, Redemption* (1994), and *Heartlove: Wedding and Love Poems* (1998).

INDEX